Falkirk, S
& Dist.
Street Atlas

CONTENTS

Area of Coverage	2-3
Key to Map Symbols	4
Aberfoyle & Avonbridge	5
Banknock & Balfron	6-7
Bathgate, Blackburn & Boghall	8-13
Bo'ness	14-17
Bonnybridge	18-21
Bridge of Allan	22-23
Broxburn & Uphall	24-27
Buchlyvie, Callander & Cowie	28-29
Denny & Dunipace	30-31
Deanston, Doune & Drymen	32-33
Dunblane	34-35
Falkirk; includes Carron, Carronshore, Hallglen, Larbert & Stenhousemuir	36-47
Fallin, Fintry & Gargunnock	48-49
Gartmore, Gartocharn & Killearn	50-51
Grangemouth; includes Laurieston & Skinflats	52-59
Kippen, Kirkliston, Newbridge & Ratho Station	60-61
Linlithgow & Linlithgow Bridge	62-63
Philpstoun, Bridgend & Plean	64-65
Polmont; inlcudes Brightons, California, Maddiston, Redding, Reddingmuirhead, Rumford, Shieldhill, Wallacestone & Westquarter	66-71
Ratho & Slamannan	72-73
South Queensferry	74-75
Stirling; includes Bannockburn	76-84
Strathblane	85
Thornhill & Torphichen	86
Westfield & Whitecross	87
Winchburgh	88

ISBN 978 1 86097 299 7

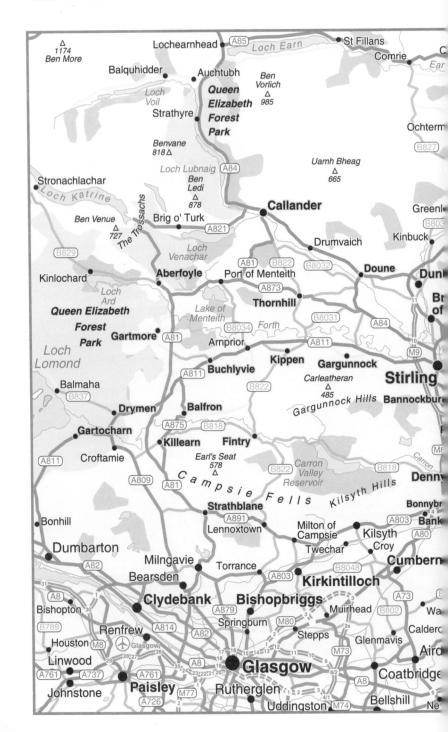

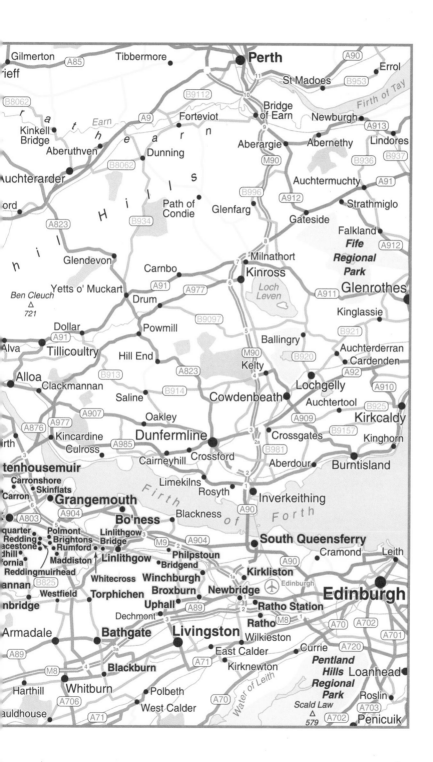

M9	Motorway
A9	Primary route dual / single carriageway
A872	A road dual / single carriageway
B816	B road dual / single carriageway
	Unclassified road
→	One way street
	Pedestrianised street
==>==	Track / path
	Railway and station
- - - -	Railway tunnel
●●●●●	Antonine Wall (course of)
●●●●●●●●	Foot ferry
◈ ◈ ◈	Police / fire / ambulance station
◈ ◈	Coastguard / lifeboat station
▲ ▼	Primary / secondary school
△	Special or independent school
+	Church / place of worship
■ ●	Notable or important building

P PO	Parking / post office
L F	Library / filling station
H S	Hospital / superstore
⚐ a	Castle / antiquity
m B	Museum / bus station
⌂ ❋	Historic house / garden
◤ i	Viewpoint / tourist information centre
✕ ✹	Battlefield / other tourist attraction
▲ ⊡	Camping / caravan site
	Woodland
	Recreation, park or cemetery
	Built-up area
	Rocks
	Shingle
	Sand
	Mud
	Loch
∼	Stream

Scale 1:14 000

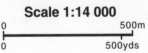

0   500m

0   500yds

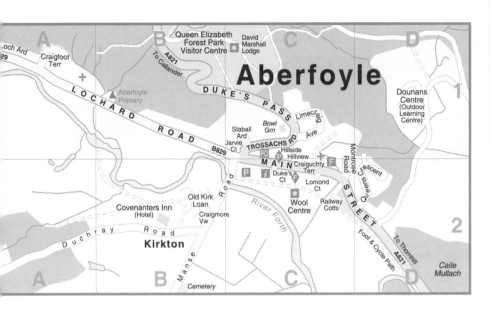

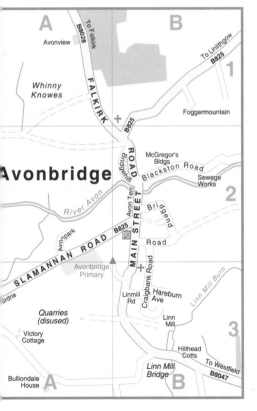

Index to Aberfoyle

Craigfoot Terrace	A1
Craigmore View	B2
Craiguchty Terrace	C1
Duchray Road	A2
Duke's Court	C2
Duke's Pass	C1
Hillside	C1
Hillview	C1
Jarvie Court	C1
Limecraig Avenue	C1
Lochard Road	A1
Lomond Court	C2
Main Street	C2
Manse Road	B2
Montrose Road	C2
Old Kirk Loan	B2
Queens Crescent	D2
Railway Cottages	C2
Staball Ard	C1
Trossachs Road	C1

Index to Avonbridge

Avon Park	A2
Avon Terrace	B2
Blackston Road	B2
Bridgend Road	B2
Bridgehill	B2
Craigbank Road	B3
Falkirk Road	A1
Hareburn Avenue	B3
Hillhead Cottages	B3
Linmill Road	B3
McGregor's Buildings	B2
Main Street	B3
Slamannan Road	A3

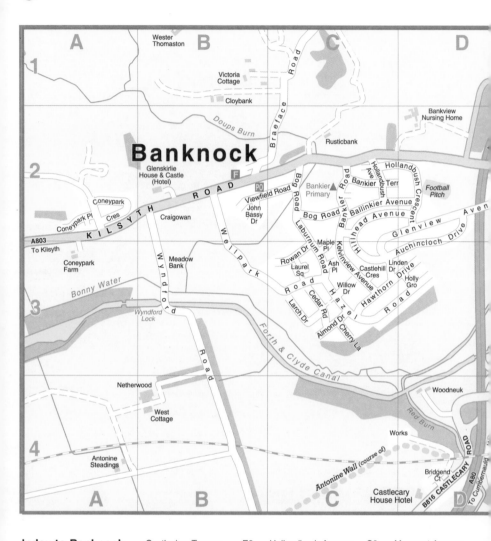

Index to Banknock

Almond Drive	C3	Castleview Terrace	E2
Anderson Terrace	F2	Cedar Road	C3
Antonine Gate	E4	Cherry Lane	C3
Ash Place	C3	Coneypark Crescent	A2
Auchincloch Drive	D3	Coneypark Place	A2
Ballinker Avenue	C2	Cumbernauld Road	E2
Bankier Road	C2	Doctors Brae	F1
Bankier Terrace	C2	Dundas Cottages	E3
Bog Road	C2	Garngrew Cottages	D2
Braeface Road	C2	Garngrew Road	D2
Bridgend Court	D4	Glasgow Road	E2
Castlecary Road	D4	Glenview Avenue	D2
Castlehill Crescent	C3	Hawthorn Drive	C3
		Hazel Road	C3
		Hillhead Avenue	C2

Hollandbush Avenue	C2	Margaret Avenue	
Hollandbush Crescent	D2	Mayfield Drive	
Holly Grove	D3	Rowan Drive	
James Street	E2	Station Road	
John Bassy Drive	B2	Thorndale Gardens	
John Street	E2	Viewfield Road	
Kelvinview Avenue	C3	Walton Road	
Kerr Crescent	E2	Wellpark Road	
Kilsyth Road	B2	Willow Drive	
Laburnum Road	C2	Wyndford Road	
Larch Drive	C3		
Laurel Square	C3		
Linden Drive	C3		
McVean Place	F1		
Maple Place	C3		

Index to Balfron

Balgair Road	C2	Roman Road	C2
Bankers Brae	B2	Shepherds Court	B2
Barnwell Drive	A2	South Lomond	B2
Buchanan Court	B2	Terrace	
Buchanan Street	B2	Spinners Street	B2
Burns Begg	C2	Spoker's Loan	B1
Crescent		Station Road	A1
Burnside	B1	Strathview Terrace	B2
Cotton Street	B1	Weavers Winnel	B1
Dominie Park	B2		
Donaldson Way	A2		
Dunkeld Court	B2		
Dunmore Street	B2		
Endrick Gardens	B2		
Endrick Road	B2		
George Terrace	B2		
Greek Thompson	A2		
Road			
Greenfield Court	B2		
Hillhead Brae	B2		
Kepculloch Road	B1		
Kiltrochan Drive	C2		
Kirkmill Road	B2		
Lomond Terrace	B2		
Moor Road	B1		
Printers Row	A3		

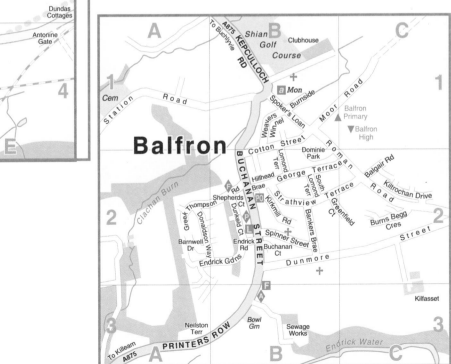

Belvedere

Belvedere Wood

Balbardie Park of Peace

Athletics Ground

To A801

A800

Bathgate Water

Chapmans Brae

Belvedere

Dykeside Road

Hillhouse Avenue

Ballencrieff Mill

Chapmans Brae

Belvedere La

Belvedere Pl

Road

Dundas Street

Turner Street

Jardine Pl

BALMUIR ROAD

Balmuir Avenue

Millhaugh La

Lothian St

Balba

Eastoun Farm

BATHGATE

Works

MILL ROAD

Mill Ct

Cochrane Rd

Balbardie Vw

Marmion

Wave

Easton Road

Milton Cotts

Burnside Road

Waverley Pl

Middlerig

Colinshiel St

Hamilton Ave

Traprain

Buchan Rd

Newlands Ct

Road

Rec Grd

South Loch Pk

Mansfield Gro

Gardens

Hamilton La

Crescent

Bathgate West Nursery School

Muir

Cess Ct

Millburn Rd

Carron Ct

A800

MILL ROAD

Cinema

North

Park

Road

Monkland Road

Irvine

A89

SOUTH BRIDG

Hope Park

Hope Pl

Wood-head Pl

Ashbank Ct

GLASGOW

ROAD

B708

Bridgend Pl

Bridgend Gdns

Recreation Ground

St Mary's RC Prim

Cairn-papple House

Menzies Road

Gardners La

Ba

A89

To Armadale

Windyknowe Primary

Windyknowe Crescent

Windyknowe Park

ROAD

Creamery Park (Football Grd)

Park

Bridgend Ct

Bathgate Cemetery

Bathgate Water

Square D3
1 Engine Pl
Square E3
2 Balgrochan
3 Helenslea

Hardhill

Durham Drive

Durham Drive

HARDHILL

Boghead Cemetery

Windyknowe

Bridgend

Meadow-park Cres

Meadowpark Ave

Dismantled R

Foundry

B708
To Armadale

SIBBALDS
BRAE

Hardhill Ave

Hardhill Terrace

Langlaud Gdns

Boghead Cres

Falside Dr

Crescent

Dalling Ave

Meadowpark Road

Meadowpark

Whitburn

Road

Paul

Garden Cottage

Falside Terrace

Falside Cresc

Robertson Ave

Bridgend

Sylvan Way

Dalling Rd

Young Cres

Dalling Rd

Malcolm Ct

WHITBURN

Falside

Whiteside Cotts

Whiteside

ROAD

Bog

Whiteside

Factory

Whiteside Ct

Whiteside

Whiteside

Teepit Hill

Whiteside Industrial Estate

Cycle Path

Avenue

Birniehill

Birniehill Rd

Standhill Ct

Boghead Burn

Whiteside Farm La

Birniehill Cres

B7002

12

Index to Bathgate & Blackburn

Academy Place	E3
Academy Street	E3
Acredale	E3
Alexandra Avenue	J3
Alexandra Drive	J3
Almond Road	F8
Almondvale Gardens	G10
Andrew Avenue	J4
Anne Street	H3
Ash Grove	G9
Ash Grove	H3
Ash Terrace	G9
Ashbank Court	B3
Athol Place	E2
Athol Terrace	E2
Avon Road	D2
Balbardie Avenue	D2
Balbardie Crescent	D2
Balbardie Road	E3
Balbardie View	D2
Balgrochan Terrace (2)	E3
Ballencrieff Mill	B1
Balmuir Avenue	C1
Balmuir Road	C2
Barrie Terrace	F3
Bathgate Road	F8
Beech Road	H3
Beechwood Gardens	G8
Beechwood Place	G8
Beechwood Road	G8
Belvedere Lane	C1
Belvedere Place	C1
Belvedere Road	C1
Birniehill Avenue	C5
Birniehill Crescent	C5
Birniehill Road	C5
Birniehill Terrace	C6
Blackburn Road	G6
Bloomfield Place	E3
Boghall Drive	H4
Boghall Farm Steadings	J4
Boghead Crescent	B4
Bridge Court	D3
Bridgend Court	C3
Bridgend Gardens	C3
Bridgend Park	C3
Bridgend Place	C3
Bruce Road	F4
Bruce Street	F5, F6
Buchan Road	C2
Bughtknowes Drive	F2
Burns Terrace	F4
Burnside Road	C2
Burnvale Avenue	F5
Cairnpapple House	D3
Carlyle Terrace	F4
Carnegie Road	J4
Carron Court	D3
Castle Place	F4
Castle Road	E6
Catherine Terrace	G8
Chapmans Brae	C1
Charles Crescent	J4
Charles Lane	J3
Cherry Avenue	H3
Church Park	E3
Church Place	E3
Cochrane Street	D2
Colinshiel Avenue	B2
Colinshiel Street	B2
Cowan Street	H4
Crosshill Drive	F3
Daisyhill Court	G9
Daisyhill Road	G10
Dalling Avenue	C4
Dalling Road	C4
Drumcross Road	F2, H1
Dundas Street	D2
Durham Avenue	B3
Durham Drive	B3
Dykeside Road	C1
East Main Street	G10
Easter Inch Road	G6
Easter Inch Steadings	G6
Easton Road	C2
Edinburgh Road	E3, H4
Elibank Court	G9
Elizabeth Drive	H3
Elizabeth Lane	J3
Elm Grove	H9
Elm Park	H9
Elm Road	J3
Elm Terrace	H8
Engine Lane	E3
Engine Place (1)	D3
Factory Road	C5
Falside Crescent	B4
Falside Drive	B4
Falside Terrace	B4
Farrier Court	G10
Fitzallan Place	E6
Fountainhead Road	E2
Galabraes Crescent	F2
Gardners Lane	D3
George Place	D3
George Street	D3
Gideon Court	E2
Gideon Street	E2
Glasgow Road	B3
Glebe Road	F3
Glen Way	E2
Glen, The	E1
Glenalmond Terrace	E1
Glenavon Terrace	E1

continued overleaf...

11

lex to Bathgate & ackburn cont...

nbare Court	F3	Limefield Lane	G3	Old Well Court	G6
ncairn Terrace	F1	Limefield Place	G3	Old Well Road	G6
nmavis Drive	E2	Limefield Road	G2	Owen Stone Street	G6
rdon Avenue	E4	Lindsay Gardens	F4	Pentland Avenue	J4
aham Court	H9	Livery Street	D2	Petershill Gardens	F2
en, The	F2	Lothian Street	D2	Philip Avenue	H3
ig Crescent	F3	MacDonald Gardens	H9	Pinewood Place	H9
milton Lane	B2	Main Street	D2	Pottishaw Place	F8
milton Road	C2	Malcolm Court	C4	Pottishaw Road	C8
hover Close	D2	Manse Place	H3	Puir Wifes Brae	G4
opy Valley Road	H10	Mansefield Court	D2	Quoiters Court	F10
rdhill Drive	B4	Mansefield Grove	D2	Race Road	B2
rdhill Road	B4	Mansefield Street	D2	Ramsay Crescent	F3
rdhill Terrace	B4	Marchwood Avenue	F3	Rattray Gardens	H10
rdy Gardens	J4	Marchwood Crescent	F4	Redhouse Court	H10
tfield Place	E2	Margaret Avenue	H3	Redhouse Place	G8
enslea	E3	Marina Road	H3	Redhouse Road	J9
ottages (3)		Marjoribanks Street	E3	Reid Crescent	E6
gh Street	E2	Marjory Court	F4	Reid Road	F6
Crescent	E2	Marjory Place	F5	Riddochill Court	E9
house Avenue	C1	Marmion Road	D2	Riddochill Crescent	F9
view Cottages	J10	Mavis Bank	E1	Riddochill Drive	F9
pe Park Gardens	B3	Mavisbank Gardens	E1	Riddochill Road	F9
pe Park	B3	Meadowpark Avenue	C4	Riddochill View	E9
oefield Drive	F9	Meadowpark	C4	Riverside Lea Crofts	J10
oefield Place	F9	Crescent		Robertson Avenue	B4
oefield Road	F9	Meadowpark Road	C4	Rockvale Cottages	J10
petoun Lane	E3	Meikle Inch Lane	E6	Rosebery Crescent	E4
petoun Street	E3	Menzies Road	D3	Rosemount Court	E3
nter Grove	H4	Meylea Street	G5	Rowan Drive	G8
h Crescent	G4	Mid Street	E3	Rowan Lane	G8
hcorse Place	F8	Mill Court	D2	Rowan Place	H8
hcross	C6	Mill Road	D2	Rowan Street	G8
hcross Drive	C7	(Bathgate)		Rowan Terrace	G9
hcross Park	B7	Mill Road	F10	Royal Scot Court	E3
hcross	C7	(Blackburn)		Russell Place	D6
teadings		Millburn Road	C3	Russell Road	D6
hmuir Road	E7	Millhaugh Lane	D2	Russell Way	D6
h Wood Avenue	G5	Milton Cottages	C2	St Mary's Place	F4
ne Crescent	C3	Monkland Road	C3	School Lane	E3
nes Young Road	E6	Mosside Court	G9	Scott Terrace	F4
rdine Place	B1	Mosside Drive	G8	Seafield Road	J9
vey Street	E2	Mosside Road	G9	Sibbalds Brae	A4
m Crescent	G4	Mosside Terrace	E6	Simpson Crescent	F4
w Gardens	E3	(Bathgate)		South Bridge Street	D3
g Street	E3	Mosside Terrace	G8	South Loch Park	D3
k Road	F4	(Blackburn)		South Mid Street	E3
kton Avenue	G4	Muir Road	C3	Spring Grove	H4
kton Court	G3	Murrayfield Drive	G9	Spring Grove	H4
kton Place	G4	Murrayfield Terrace	G9	Cottages	
deside Avenue	F9	Napier Avenue	F3	Standhill Court	C5
deside Drive	F9	Neilson Court	E9	Standhill Road	C6
deside Gardens	E9	Newland Avenue	E3	Starlaw Avenue	H4
deside Road	F9	Newlands Court	C2	Starlaw Crescent	J4
ngfauld Gardens	B4	Norman Court	G10	Starlaw Gardens	H4
chburn View	F10	North Bridge Street	D3	Starlaw Road	J4
dand Road	E6	Northbank Cottages	E2	Starlaw Terrace	H4
defield Crescent	H3	Old Hallknowe Court	F6	Starlaw Walk	H4
		Old Hallknowe Place	F5	Steelyard, The	D3
		Old Hallknowe	F6	Stevenson Terrace	F4
		Terrace		Strand Drive	C8

Stuart Court	F4
Stuart Terrace	F4
Sunnyside Avenue	F2
Sutherland Crescent	E4
Sycamore Walk	G9
Sylvan Way	C4
Tollbraes Road	G5
Torphichen Road	E1
Torphichen Street	E2
Traprain Crescent	C2
Turf Place	F9
Turner Street	D2
Union Road	E3
Veterans Cottages	F3
Wallace Road	F4
Waverley Place	D2
Waverley Street	D2
Weaver Place	E2
West Main Street	E10
Whitburn Road	B6, C4
Whitehill Drive	F9
Whitehill Road	F8
Whitehill View	F9
Whitelaw Drive	H3
Whiteside	C5
Whiteside	C5
Cottages	
Whiteside Court	C5
Whiteside Farm	A5
Lane	
Whitestone Place	F8
Windyknowe	B3
Crescent	
Windyknowe Park	B3
Woodhead Place	B3
Young Crescent	C4
Yule Place	F8
Yule Terrace	F9

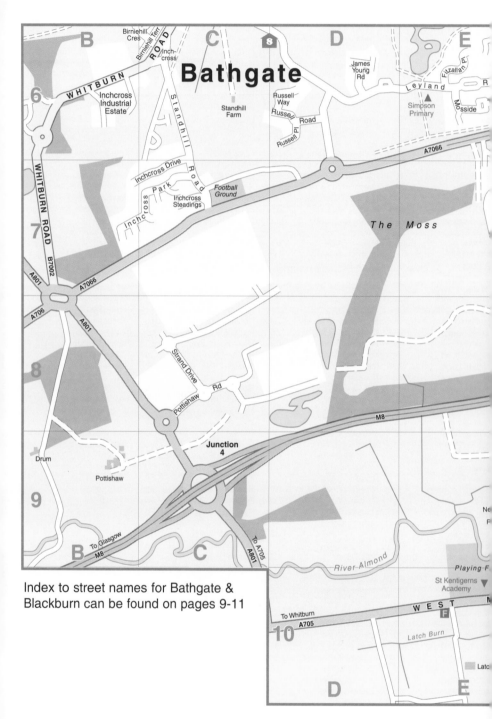

Index to street names for Bathgate &
Blackburn can be found on pages 9-11

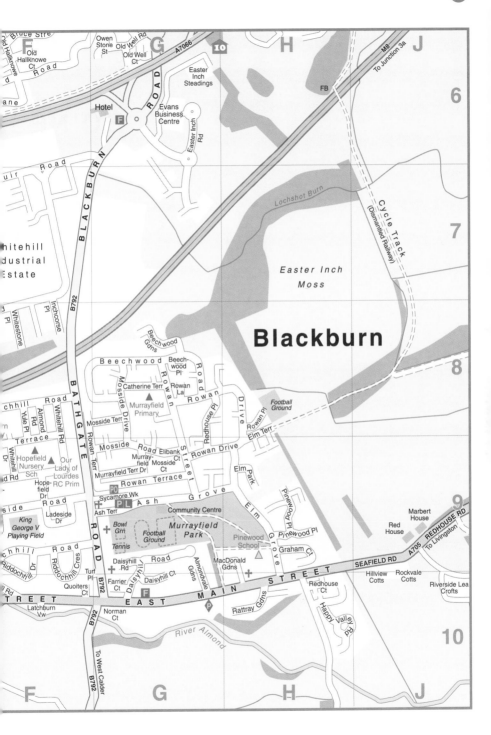

Blackburn

Easter Inch Moss

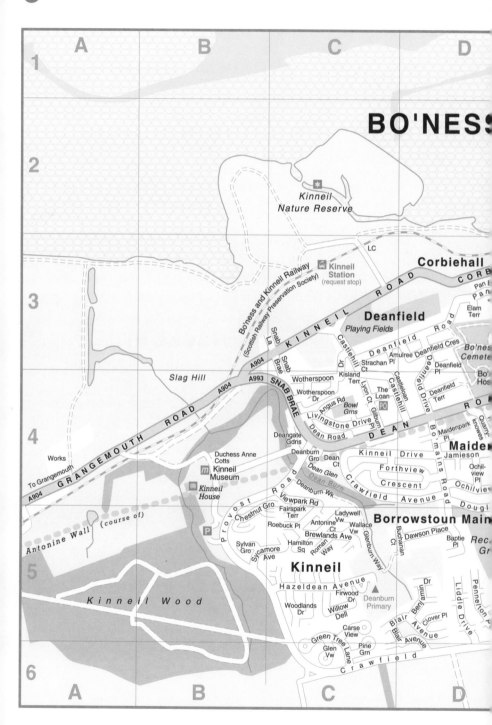

BO'NESS

Kinneil
Nature Reserve

LC

Kinneil
Station
(request stop)

Corbiehall

CORB

Bo'ness and Kinneil Railway
(Scottish Railway Preservation Society)

KINNEIL ROAD

Deanfield
Playing Fields

Pan E
Pan

Elam
Terr

Deanfield Road

Amulree Deanfield Cres

Bo'ness
Cemete

Slag Hill

A904

Snab Brae
Snab La

A993

A904

SNAB BRAE

Wotherspoon

Wotherspoon
Dr

Angus Rd

Castlehill
Dr

Kisland
Terr

Strachan Pl

Lyon Ct

Deanfield
Ct

The Loan

Gilburn Pl
Castlehill

Deanfield
Pl

Deanfield
Terr

Deanfield Drive

Castlehill

PO

Bo'
Hos

RO

GRANGEMOUTH ROAD

Works

To Grangemouth

A904

Bowl
Grns

Livingstone Drive

Dean Road

DEAN

Maidenpark Pl

Quarry
knowes

Bo'mans Road

Maide

Jamieson

Ochil-
view
Pl

Ochilvie

Dougl

Deangate
Gdns

Deanburn
Gro

Dean
Ct

Kinneil Drive

Forthview

Crescent

Dean Glen

Dean Burn

Crawfield Avenue

Duchess Anne
Cotts

Kinneil
Museum

Kinneil
House

Deanburn Wk

Provost Road

Viewpark Rd

Fairspark
Terr

Roebuck Pl

Chestnut Gro

Antonine
Ct

Ladywell
Vw

Wallace
Vw

Brewlands Ave

Hamilton
Sq

Roman
Way

Glenburn Way

Borrowstoun Main

Buchanan
Ct

Dawson Place

Baptie
Pl

Rec
Gr

Antonine Wall (course of)

P

Sylvan
Gro

Sycamore
Ave

Kinneil

Hazeldean Avenue

Kinneil Wood

Woodlands
Dr

Willow
Dell

Firwood
Dr

Deanburn
Primary

Carse
View

Green Tree Lane

Glen
Vw

Pine
Grn

Crawfield

Blair

Benjamin

Dr

Blair Avenue

Clover Pl

Blair Avenue

Liddle Drive

Pennelton P

E   F   G   H

1

West Pier   East Pier

E2
ands Close
's Wynd
Street
ton Lane
t Street
ter Street

Harbour

Lock   Dock

Scottish National Railway Museum

Bo'ness Station

Grangepans

Bridgeness

Bo'ness Motor Museum

2

UNION STREET

Waggon Rd
Pier St
Comm-issioner St
Union Ct

Seaview
North
South
Salmon
Street
Provi-dence Brae
Brae

Main St
DOCK ST
A904
Links Ct
Links Court Ind Estate

Thirlestane Pl

Thirlestane Man o' War Way

Dower Cres

Haney's Way

Works

Furnace La The Tower Gdns

BRIDGENESS ROAD

Craigfoot Terr
Craig Vw
Philping-stone La

Bowl Grn

Bridgeness La

Avenue
Town Hall
School Brae
Glebe Park
Braehead Gro
Braehead

LINKS ROAD

Bomar Ave The Boo
Old St Mary's La

Stewart Avenue

Links Braes

Bo'ness Public School

Stark's Brae

GRANGEPANS

Links Pl
Park
Victoria Pl
Cairn's La

Rattray St
Docoot Brae
Cowdenhill Rd

Craigfoot Terr

Philping-stone La
The Run

Bridge-ness Cres
South Philpingstone La

3

Stewart
Marchlands La
Cadzow La
Darian La
Marchlands Terr

Grange Terrace

Victoria Park

Grange Loan

Grange Primary

Fountainpark Cres

Harbour Road

Kinningars Park

Tidings Hill
Cadzow

Dugald Stewart Ave
Marchlands Ave
James Watt Ave
Kelty Ave
Erngath Rd
Erngath Road

Grahams Ave

Bowl Grn

Grahamsdyke La

Pier Rd

Bridgeness

Douglas Park

DEAN ROAD

Viewforth

GRAHAMSDYKE

Kinglass Rd
Kinglass Park
Gauze Rd
Kinglass Ave

School Vw
Craigallan Park

Grahamsdyke Terr

Seton Terr

Graham Crescent

Drumside Terr

Drum Cotts
Acre
View Pl

A706

Lothian Cres
St Mary's RC Primary

Roman Camp (site of)

Academy Road

Grahamsdyke Pl

Hadrian Way

park Ave
Drum Ave

Drum Road
A993

Wheat-field Rd
Hillside
Farm-stead Way
Grove
Drum Farm La

4

16

LINLITHGOW

Clydesdale Street
George
Newtown Cotts
Baker Street
Comrie Terr

Cadzow Road

Newtown

Grahamsdyke

The Academy

Playing Fields

Drumpark Ave

Drumacre Rd

Muirend Ct

Longacre

Newtown
Birkhill
Birk-hill St
Crescent
Hillcrest

Muirepark Ct
Avenue
Mingle Place

Kinglass Centre

Recreation Centre

Gauze e
Gauze Ct

Kinglass Ct

Kinglass Drive
Bonhard Ct
Bonhard Way
Drumview Gdns

5

Barony Ct
Jessfield Pl
Northbank Pl
Northbank Ct
Northbank Dr
Northbank Pk
Redbrae Ave

Borrowstoun Road

Kinglass Pk

Kinglass Cottage

Northbank

Redbrae Cottages

The Barony Theatre
Crosshill Dr
Shafto Pl
St John's Way
Ritchie Place
Braefoot Road
Cathrine Gro

Howieson Ave
Henry St

Bonhard Cottages

Borrowstoun

A706
To Linlithgow

West Lothian Golf Course

Bonhard House

6

E   F   G   H

Index to street names can be found overleaf

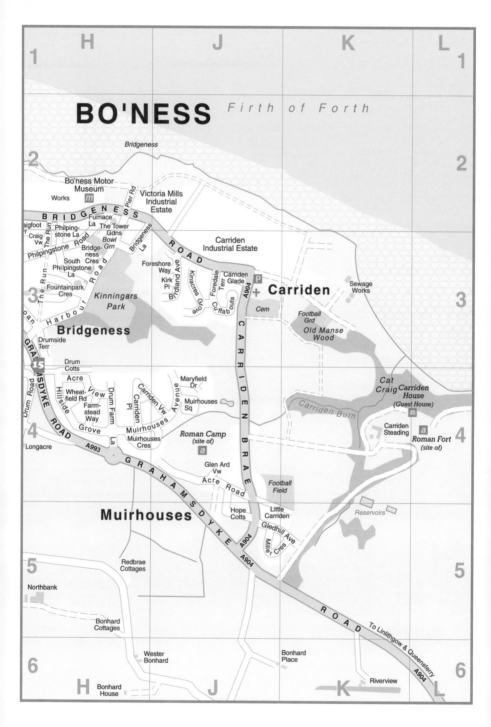

BO'NESS

Firth of Forth

Bridgeness

Bo'ness Motor Museum

Works

Victoria Mills Industrial Estate

B R I D G E N E S S

Pier Rd

Furnace La

The Tower Gdns

Philping- stone La

aigfoot

Craig Vw

The Run

Philpingstone Road

Bowl Grn

Bridge- ness Cres

Bridgeness La

Carriden Industrial Estate

South Philpingstone La

Foreshore Way

Carriden Glade

R O A D

Fountainpark Cres

Harbour Road

Kinningars Park

Kirk Pl

Birtland Ave

Kinacres Grove

Foredale Terr

Carriden Terr

Cuffabouts

Carriden

Cem

Sewage Works

Bridgeness

Drumside Terr

Football Grd

Old Manse Wood

Drum Cotts

Acre

Wheat- field Rd

View

Drum Farm

Carriden Vw

Maryfield Dr

Muirhouses Sq

Cat Craig

Carriden House (Guest House)

Hillside

Farm- stead Way

Carriden Pl

Carriden Brae

Carriden Steading

Grove

Muirhouses

Roman Fort (site of)

Muirhouses Cres

Roman Camp (site of)

Carriden Burn

Longacre

A993

Glen Ard Vw

Football Field

Reservoirs

Muirhouses

G R A H A M S D Y K E

Acre Road

Hope Cotts

Little Carriden

A904

Gledhill Ave

Miller Cres

Redbrae Cottages

R O A D

To Linlithgow & Queensferry

Northbank

Bonhard Cottages

Wester Bonhard

Bonhard Place

A904

Riverview

Bonhard House

Index to Bo'ness

Place	Grid	Place	Grid	Place	Grid	Place	Grid
Academy Road	F3	Crawfield Lane	E5	Grahamsdyke Road	G3	Newtown	E4
Acre Road	J4	Crawfield Road	C6	Grahamsdyke	G4	Newtown Cottages	E4
Acre View	H4	Crosshill Drive	E5	Terrace		Newtown Street	E4
Amulree Place	C2	Cuffabouts	J3	Grange Loan	G3	North Street	E2
Angus Street	C4	Darian Lane	E3	Grange Terrace	F3	Northbank Court	F5
Antonine Court	C5	Dawson Place	D5	Grangemouth Road	A4	Northbank Drive	F5
Avon Place	E3	Dean Court	C4	Grangepans	G3	Northbank Park	E5
Back Hill	D3	Dean Road	C4, F3	Green Tree Lane	C5	Ochilview Place	D4
Baker Street	E4	Deanburn Grove	C4	Hadrian Way	G4	Ochilview Road	D4
Baptie Place	D5	Deanburn Walk	C4	Hamilton Lane (4)	E2	Ochilview Terrace	D4
Barony Court	E5	Deanfield Crescent	D3	Hamilton Square	C5	Old St Mary's Lane	F2
Benjamin Drive	E5	Deanfield Drive	D3	Haney's Way	G2	Pan Braes	D3
Birdland Avenue	J3	Deanfield Place	D3	Harbour Road	H3	Panbrae Road	D3
Birkhill Crescent	E4	Deanfield Road	C3	Hazeldean Avenue	C5	Park Lane	G3
Birkhill Street	E4	Deanfield Terrace	D4	Henry Street	F5	Pennelton Place	D5
Blair Avenue	C5	Deangate Gardens	C4	Hillcrest	E4	Philpingstone Lane	H3
Bog, The	F2	Dock Street	F2	Hillside Grove	H4	Philpingstone Road	G3
Bo'mains Road	D4	Doocot Brae	G3	Hope Cottages	J5	Pier Road	H2
Bomar Avenue	E2	Douglas Drive	D4	Hope Street (3)	E2	Pine Green	C6
Bonhard Cottages	H5	Douglas Place	E4	Howieson Avenue	E5	Providence Brae	E2
Bonhard Court	G4	Douglas Road	E4	James Watt Avenue	F3	Provost Road	B5
Bonhard Way	G4	Douglas Terrace	E4	Jamieson Avenue	D4	Quarryknowes, The	D4
Borrowstoun Crescent	E5	Dower Crescent	G2	Jeffrey Bank	E3	Rattray Street	G2
Borrowstoun Road	E5	Drum Cottages	G4	Jessfield Place	E5	Redbrae Avenue	F5
Borrowstoun Place	E5	Drum Farm Lane	H4	Kelty Avenue	F3	Redbrae Cottages	H5
Boundary Street	G2	Drum Road	G4	Kinacres Grove	J3	Register Street (6)	E2
Braefoot Road	F5	Drumacre Road	G4	Kinglass Avenue	F3	Richmond Terrace	D3
Braehead	E3	Drumpark Avenue	G4	Kinglass Court	F4	Ritchie Place	F5
Braehead Grove	E3	Drumside Terrace	H3	Kinglass Drive	F5	Roebuck Place	C5
Brewlands Avenue	C5	Drumview Gardens	F5	Kinglass Park	F5	Roman Way	C5
Bridgeness Crescent	H3	Duchess Anne Cottages	B4	Kinneil Drive	C4	Run,The	H3
Bridgeness Lane	H3	Dugald Stewart Avenue	F3	Kinneil Road	C3	St John's Way	E5
Bridgeness Road	H2	Dundas Street	D3	Kirk Place	J3	Salmon Court	E2
Buchanan Court	D5	East Pier Street	E2	Kisland Terrace	C4	School Brae	E2
Cadzow Crescent	E3	Elam Terrace	D3	Ladywell View	C5	School View	F3
Cadzow Avenue	E4	Erngath Road	F3	Liddle Drive	D5	Scotlands Close (1)	E2
Cadzow Lane	E3	Ewart Grove	E5	Links Braes	F2	Seaview Place	E2
Cairn's Lane	G3	Fairspark Terrace	C5	Links Court	F2	Seton Terrace	G3
Carriden Brae	J3	Farmstead Way	H4	Links Place	G3	Shafto Place	E5
Carriden Glade	J3	Firwood Drive	C5	Links Road	F2	Snab Brae	C3
Carriden Place	H4	Foredale Terrace	J3	Linlithgow Road	E3, E4	Snab Lane	C3
Carriden View	H4	Foreshore Way	J3	Little Carriden	J4	South Street	E2
Carse View	C5	Forthview Crescent	C4	Livingstone Drive	C4	South Philpingstone Lane	H3
Castlehill	C3, C4	Fountainpark Crescent	H3	Loan, The	C4	Stark's Brae	F3
Castleloan	C4	Furnace Lane	H2	Lothian Crescent	F4	Stewart Avenue	E3, F2
Cathrine Grove	F5	Gauze Court	F4	Lothian Street	F4	Strachan Court	C3
Chestnut Grove	B5	Gauze Place	F4	Lyon Court	C4	Sycamore Avenue	B5
Church Road	D3	Gauze Road	F3, F5	Maidenpark Place	D4	Sylvan Grove	B5
Church Wynd	E3	George Street	E4	Main Street	F2	Thirlestane	G2
Clover Place	D5	Gibson's Wynd (2)	E2	Man o' War Way	G2	Thirlestane Place	G2
Clydesdale Street	E4	Gilburn Place	C4	Marchlands Avenue	F3	Tower Gardens, The	H2
Commissioner Street	F2	Gledhill Avenue	J5	Marchlands Lane	F3	Union Court	F2
Comrie Terrace	E4	Glen Ard View	J4	Marchlands Terrace	E3	Union Street	E2
Corbiehall	D3	Glen View	C6	Market Street (5)	E2	Victoria Place	G3
Cowdenhill Road	G2	Glenburn Way	C5	Maryfield Drive	J4	Viewforth	F3
Craig View	H3	Graham Crescent	G3	Miller Crescent	J5	Viewpark Road	C4
Craigallan Park	F3	Grahamsdyke Avenue	G3	Mingle Place	F4	Waggon Road	E2
Craigfoot Terrace	G2	Grahamsdyke Lane	G3	Muirend Court	G4	Wallace View	C5
Crawfield Avenue	C4	Grahamsdyke Place	F4	Muirepark Court	E4	Wheatfield Road	H4
				Muirhouses Avenue	H4	Willow Dell	C5
				Muirhouses Crescent	H4	Woodlands Drive	C5
				Muirhouses Square	J4	Wotherspoon Drive	C4

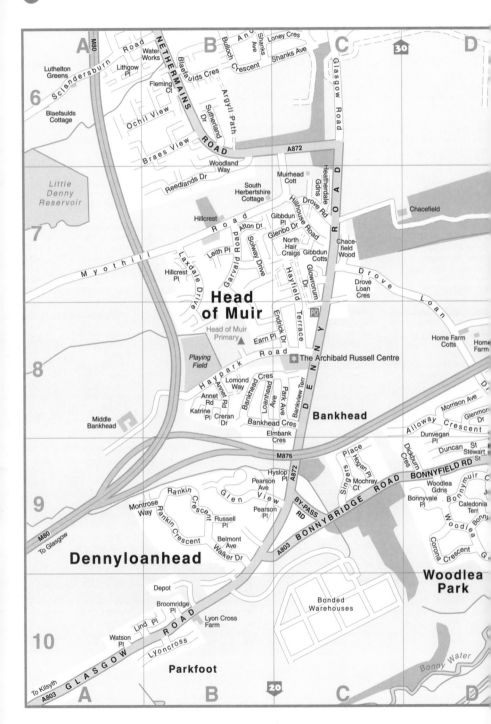

Head of Muir

Bankhead

Dennyloanhead

Woodlea Park

Parkfoot

Chacefield

Home Farm
Cotts

Home Farm

Chacefield Wood

Drove Loan

Drove Loan Cres

Luthelton Greens

Blaefaulds Cottage

Little Denny Reservoir

Water Works

Lithgow Pl

Fleming Ct

Ochil View

Braes View

Blaefaulds Cres

Sutherland Dr

Argyll Path

Bulloch Crescent

Shanks Ave

Loney Cres

Shanks Ave

Glasgow Road

A872

Woodland Way

Reedlands Dr

Muirhead Cott

Heatherdale Gdns

Drove Rd

Hillhouse Road

South Herbertshire Cottage

Hillcrest

Myothill

Hillcrest Pl

Laxdale Drive

Garvald Road

Afton Dr

Leith Pl

Solway Drive

Gibbdun Pl

Glenbo Dr

North Hair Craigs

Gibbdun Cotts

Glowrorum Dr

Hayfield Terrace

Earn Pl

Endrick Dr

Head of Muir Primary ▲

Playing Field

Road

The Archibald Russell Centre ✴

PO

Haypark

Lomond Way

Annet Rd

Annet Rd

Bankhead Cres

Lomonhead Ave

Park Ave

Bankview Terr

Katrine Pl

Creran Dr

Bankhead Cres

Elmbank Cres

Middle Bankhead

M876

A872

Hyslop Pl

Pearson Ave

Pearson Pl

Glen View

Rankin Crescent

Montrose Way

Rankin Crescent

Russell Pl

Belmont Ave

Walker Dr

Singers Place

Hogan Pl

Mochray Ct

BY-PASS RD

BONNYBRIDGE ROAD

A803

Morrison Ave

Glenmor Dr

Alloway Crescent

Dunvegan Pl

Duncan St

Stewart St

Dickburn Cres

BONNYFIELD RD

Woodlea Gdns

Bonnyvale Pl

Bonnymuir Pl

Caledonia Terr

Woodlea

Corona Crescent

M80 To Glasgow

Depot

Broomridge Pl

Lind Pl

Watson Pl

GLASGOW ROAD

Lyoncross

Lyon Cross Farm

Bonded Warehouses

Bonny Water

To Kilsyth A803

30

20

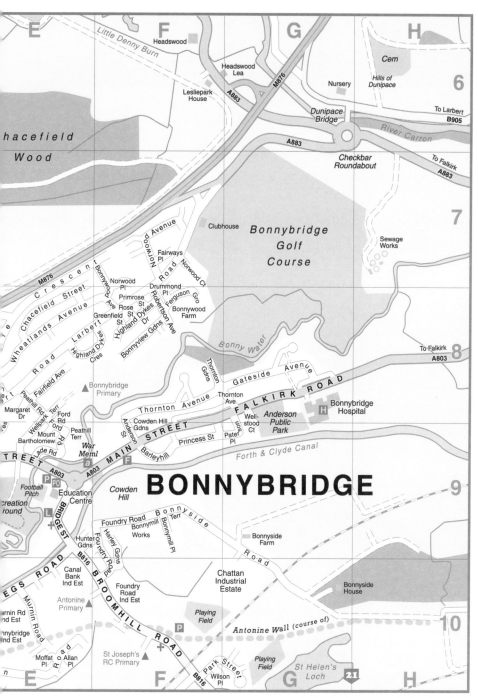

E — Little Denny Burn — Headswood

Headswood Lea

Lesliepark House

Chacefield Wood

M876 A883

Nursery

Hills of Dunipace

Cem

Dunipace Bridge

A883

To Larbert B905

River Carron

Checkbar Roundabout

To Falkirk A883

6

Clubhouse

Bonnybridge Golf Course

Sewage Works

7

M876

Chacefield Street

Wheatlands Avenue

Norwood Avenue

Fairways Pl

Norwood Rd

Norwood Ct

Drummond Pl

Ferguson Gro

Bonnywood Farm

Norwood Pl

Primrose St

Rose St

Greenfield St

Robertson Ave

Bonnyview Gdns

Highland Dykes Dr

Larbert Rd

Bonnywood Ave

Crescent

Road

Highland Dykes Cres

Bonny Water

To Falkirk A803

8

Fairfield Ave

Peathill Rd

Wellpark Terr

Margaret Dr

Ford Rd

Ford

Peathill Terr

Mount Bartholomew

Lade Rd

Ford

▲ Bonnybridge Primary

Thornton Gdns

Thornton Avenue

Cowden Hill Gdns

Anderson St

MAIN STREET

Thornton Ave

Gateside Avenue

FALKIRK ROAD

Wellstood Ct

Anderson Public Park

H Bonnybridge Hospital

Princess St

Pater St

Barleyhill

Forth & Clyde Canal

STREET

A803

War Meml

a

A803

F

BONNYBRIDGE

9

P PO

Football Pitch

Education Centre

Cowden Hill

Foundry Road

Bonnyside Terr

Bonnyside Farm

creation round

L

BRIDGE ST

Hunter Gdns

Harley Gdns

Bonnymill Works

Bonnymill Pl

Bonnyside Road

B816

FOUNDRY ROAD

BROOMHILL ROAD

Canal Bank Ind Est

Foundry Road Ind Est

Chattan Industrial Estate

Bonnyside House

LEGS ROAD

Murnin Rd Ind Est

▲ Antonine Primary

Playing Field

P

Antonine Wall (course of)

10

Murnin Road

nybridge Ind Est

Road

Moffat Pl

Allan Pl

▲ St Joseph's RC Primary

B816

Park Street

Playing Field

St Helen's Loch

21

Wilson Pl

E

F

G

H

Index to street names can be found overleaf

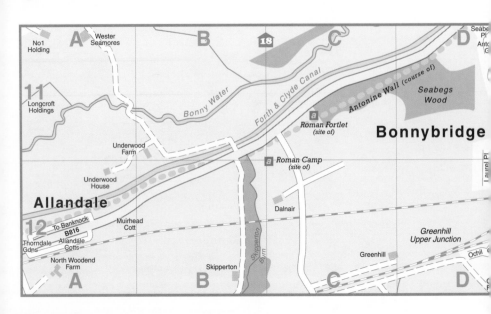

Index to Bonnybridge

Afton Drive	B7	Bridge Street	E9	Falkirk Road		
Allan Place	E10	Broomhill Road	F10	Ferguson Grove		
Allandale Cottages	A12	Broomridge Place	B10	Fleming Court		
Alloway Crescent	D8	Broomside Road	F11	Ford Road		
Anderson Street	F9	Bulloch Crescent	B6	Foundry Road		
Annet Road	B8	By-Pass Road	C9	Foxdale Avenue		
Antonine Grove	D11	Caledonia Terrace	D9	Foxdale Court		
Ardgay Crescent	E11	Chacefield Street	E8	Foxdale Drive		
Ardgay Drive	E11	Chacefield Wood	C7	Foxdale Place		
Ardgay Road	E11	Church Street	G11	Garvald Road		
Argyll Path	B6	Claremont Street	D8	Gateside Avenue		
Ashley Street	D8	Corona Crescent	D9	Gibbdun Cottages		
Atrium Way	E11	Cowan Street	E8	Gibbdun Place		
Balfour Street	D8	Cowden Hill Gardens	F9	Glasgow Road	A10,
Bankhead Crescent	B8	Creran Drive	B8	Glen View		
Bankview Terrace	C8	Denny Road	C8	Glenbo Drive		
Banton Place	E11	Dickburn Crescent	D9	Glenmore Drive		
Barleyhill	F9	Drove Loan Crescent	C7	Glenyards Road		
Belmont Avenue	B9	Drove Loan	C7	Glowrorum Drive		
Blaefaulds Crescent	B6	Drove Road	C7	Grahamsdyke Crescent		
Bonnybridge Road	C9	Drummond Place	F8	Grahamsdyke Road		
Bonnyfield Road	D9	Duncairn Avenue	D8	Greenacre Drive		
Bonnyhill Road	G11	Duncan Street	D9	Greenacre Place		
Bonnymill Place	F9	Dunure Crescent	E9	Greenacre Road		
Bonnymill Terrace	F9	Dunure Street	E9	Greenfield Street		
Bonnymuir Crescent	D9	Dunvegan Place	D9	Greenhill Court		
Bonnyside Road	F9	Earn Place	B8	Greenhill Road		
Bonnyvale Place	D9	Elmbank Crescent	B8	Greenhill Square		
Bonnyview Gardens	F8	Emma's Way	D9	Harley Gardens		
Bonnywood Avenue	F7	Endrick Drive	C8	Hayfield Terrace		
Bowling Green Place	D9	Fairfield Avenue	E8	Haypark Road		
Braes View	B6	Fairways Place	F7	Heatherdale Gardens		

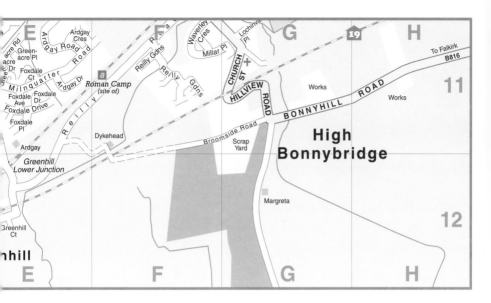

n Street	E9	Mochray Court	C9	Russell Place	B9
nland Dykes Crescent	E8	Moffat Place	E10	Sclandersburn Road	A6
nland Dykes Drive	F8	Montrose Way	B9	Seabegs Crescent	E10
crest Place	B7	Morrison Avenue	D8	Seabegs Place	D11
iouse Road	C7	Mount Bartholomew	E9	Seabegs Road	E10
iew Road	G11	Murnin Road	E10	Shanks Avenue	B6
ian Place	C9	Myothill Road	A7	Singers Place	C9
epark Terrace	D8	Nethermains Road	B6	Skene Street	E8
ter Gardens	E9	North Hair Craigs	C7	Solway Drive	B7
Jop Place	C9	Norwood Avenue	F7	Spence Street	E8
lee Way	D9	Norwood Court	F7	Stewart Street	D9
ine Place	B8	Norwood Place	F7	Sutherland Drive	B6
e Road	E9	Ochil Gardens	D12	Thorndale Gardens	A12
ert Road	E8	Ochil View	A6	Thornton Avenue	F8
rel Grove	E11	Park Avenue	C8	Thornton Gardens	F8
rel Place	D12	Park House	D9	Ure Crescent	E8
relbank Avenue	E11	Park Street	G10	Vale of Bonny View	D9
dale Drive	B7	Parkfoot	A10	Walker Drive	B9
park Drive	D11	Paterson Place	G8	Watson Place	A10
n Place	B7	Pearson Avenue	B9	Waverley Crescent	F11
I Place	A10	Pearson Place	B9	Wellpark Terrace	E9
gow Place	A6	Peathill Road	E8	Wellstood Court	G8
nhead Avenue	B8	Peathill Terrace	E9	Wheatlands Avenue	E8
ninvar Place	G12	Primrose Street	F8	Wilson Place	F10
iond Way	B8	Princess Street	F9	Woodburn Crescent	D11
ey Crescent	C6	Rankin Crescent	B9	Woodland Way	B6
ncross	B10	Reedlands Drive	B7	Woodlea Gardens	D9
n Street	F9	Reilly Gardens	F11		
anfield Avenue	D10	Reilly Road	E11		
garet Drive	E8	Robertson Avenue	F8		
ar Place	F11	Roman Road	E10		
iquarter Road	E11	Rose Street	F8		

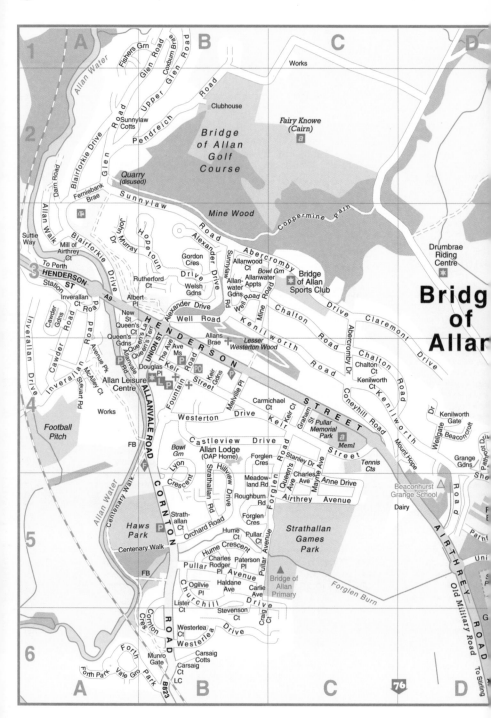

BRIDGE OF ALLAN

A 1 B 1 C 1 D

Allan Water
Fishers Grn
Glen Road
Coburn Brae
Upper Glen Road
Pendreich Road
Works
Clubhouse
Sunnylaw Cotts
Blairforkie Drive
Glen Road
Fairy Knowe (Cairn)
Dam Road
Bridge of Allan Golf Course
Quarry (disused)
Ferniebank Brae
Allan Walk
Suttie Way
Mill of Airthrey Ct
To Perth
Sunnylaw
Road
Mine Wood
Coppermine Path
Drumbrae Riding Centre
John Murray Dr
Hopetoun
Alexander Drive
Sunnylaw Rd
Abercromby Road
Allanwood Ct
Bowl Grn
Allanwater Appts
Bridge of Allan Sports Club
Bridg of Allar
HENDERSON ST
Station
Inverallan Ct
Gordon Cres
Rutherford Ct
Welsh Gdns
Drive
Allanwater Gdns
Mine Road
Well Road
Chalton Road
Claremont Drive
Abercromby Dr
Chalton Ct
Kenilworth Ct
Cawder Gdns
Cawder Road
Avenue Pk
McAlley Ct
Stewart Rd
Inverallan Drive
Inverallan Road
A9
Albert Pl
New St
Queen's Ct
Queen's Gdns
Queen's Ter
The Ave
Alexander Drive
Well Road
Allans Brae
Lesser Westerton Wood
Kenilworth Road
Coneyhill Road
Kenilworth Road
Chalton Road
Kenilworth Gate
Beaconcroft
Wellgate
Dr
HENDERSON STREET
Keir Ms
Douglas Pl
Allan Leisure Centre
ALLANVALE ROAD
Fountain Road
Keir Street
PO
Keir Gdns
Melville Pl
Carmichael Ct
Keir Street
Graham Ct
Pullar Memorial Park
Meml
STREET
Mount Hope
Grange Gdns
She
Works
Football Pitch
CORTON ROAD
Centenary Walk
Allan Water
FB
Bowl Grn
Lyon Crescent
Westerton Drive
Castleview Drive
Allan Lodge (OAP Home)
Strathallan Rd
Hillview Drive
Forglen Cres
Stanley Dr
Queen's Ave
Charles Ave
Mayne Ave
Anne Drive
Airthrey Avenue
Tennis Cts
Beaconhurst Grange School
Dairy
AIRTHREY
Haws Park
Strathallan Ct
Orchard Road
Meadowland Rd
Roughburn Rd
Forglen Cres
Hume Ct
Pullar Ct
Forglen Road
Pullar Avenue
Strathallan Games Park
Uni
S Pl
FB
Churchill Road
Hume Crescent
Charles Rodger Pl
Paterson Pl
Pullar Avenue
Bridge of Allan Primary
Forglen Burn
Old Military Road
G
Corton Cres
Ogilvie Pl
Haldane Ave
Lister Ct
Carlie Ave
Stevenson Ct
Craig Drive
Westerlea Drive
Westerlea Ct
Munro Gate
Forth Park
Vale Gro
Forth Park
B823
Carsaig Cotts
Carsaig Ct
LC
Pathfoot Drive
E
Pathf
Road
To Stirling

A B 76 C D

Index to Bridge of Allan

Abercromby Drive	C3	Inverallan Court	A3
Airthrey Avenue	C5	Inverallan Drive	A4
Airthrey Road	D5	Inverallan Road	A4
Albert Place	A3	John Murray Drive	A3
Alexander Drive	B3	Keir Court	C4
Allan Walk	A3	Keir Gardens	B4
Allans Brae	B4	Keir Street	B4
Allanvale Road	B4	Kenilworth Court	C4
Allanwater Apartments	B3	Kenilworth Gate	D4
Allanwater Gardens	B3	Kenilworth Road	C4
Allanwood Court	B3	Lister Court	B5
Anne Drive	C5	Logie Lane	D4
Avenue Mews	B4	Lyon Crescent	B5
Avenue Park	A4	McAlley Court	A4
Avenue, The	B4	Mayne Avenue	C5
Beaconcroft	D4	Meadowland Road	B5
Blairforkie Drive	A2	Melville Place	B4
Carlie Avenue	B5	Mill of Airthrey Court	A3
Carmichael Court	B4	Mine Road	B3
Carsaig Cottages	B6	Mount Hope	D4
Carsaig Court	B6	Munro Gate	B6
Castleview Drive	B4	New Street	A3
Causeway, The	E6	Ogilvie Place	B5
Cawder Gardens	A3	Orchard Road	B5
Cawder Road	A4	Paterson Place	B5
Centenary Walk	A5	Pathfoot Avenue	D4
Chalton Court	C4	Pathfoot Road	D5
Chalton Road	C3	Pathfoot Drive	D4
Charles Avenue	C5	Pendreich Road	B2
Charles Rodger Place	B5	Pendreich Way	E5
Churchill Drive	B5	Pullar Avenue	B5
Claremont Drive	C3	Pullar Court	B5
Coneyhill Road	C4	Queen's Avenue	C5
Coppermine Path	C3	Queen's Court (Bridge of Allan)	A3
Cornton Crescent	B6	Queen's Court (University)	E6
Cornton Road	B5	Queen's Gardens	A4
Coxburn Brae	B1	Queen's Lane	A4
Craig Court	B6	Queen's Terrace	A4
Darn Road	A2	Roughburn Road	B5
Douglas Place	B4	Rutherford Court	B3
East Link Road	E6	Sheriffmuir Road	E4
Ferniebank Brae	A2	Stanley Drive	C4
Fishers Green	A1	Station Road	A3
Forglen Crescent	B4	Steuart Road	A4
Forglen Road	C5	Stevenson Court	B6
Forth Park	A6	Strathallan Court	B5
Fountain Road	B4	Strathallan Road	B4
George Forrest Walk, The	E5	Sunnylaw Cottages	A2
Glen Road	A2	Sunnylaw Road	B3
Gordon Crescent	B3	Suttie Way	A3
Graham Street	C4	Union Street	B4
Grange Gardens	D4	University Road West	D5
Grange Road	D5	Upper Glen Road	B2
Haldane Avenue	B5	Vale Grove	A6
Henderson Street	A3, B3	Well Road	B3
Henry Milne Walk	E6	Wellgate Drive	D4
Hermitage Road	E5	Welsh Gardens	B3
Hillview Drive	B5	West Link Road	E6
Hopetoun Drive	B3	Westerlea Court	B6
Hume Court	B5	Westerlea Drive	B6
Hume Crescent	B5	Westerton Drive	B4

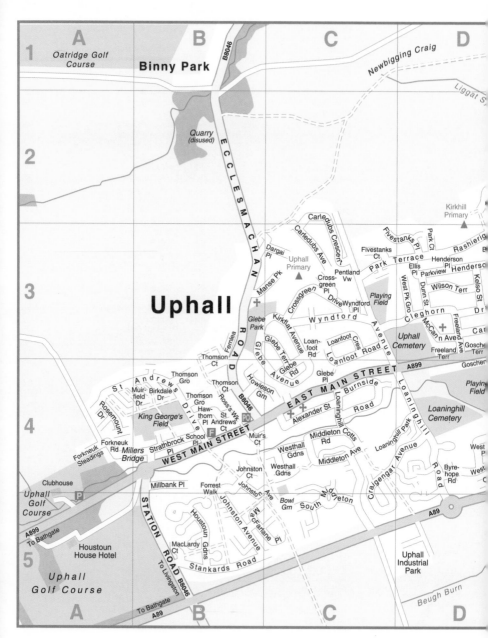

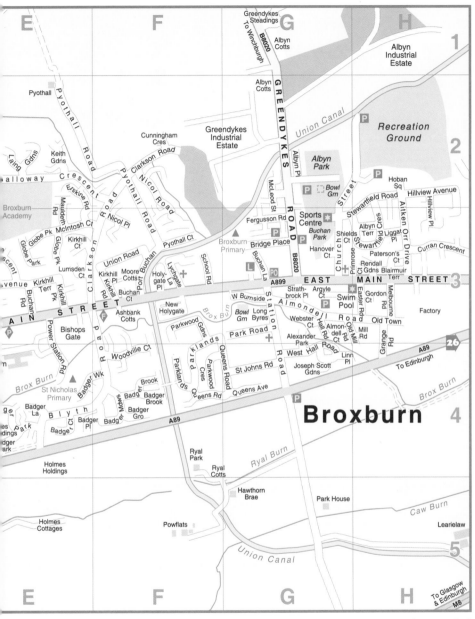

E F G H

1

Greendykes
Steadings
Albyn
Cotts

Albyn
Industrial
Estate

Pyothall

Albyn
Cotts

Union Canal

Recreation
Ground

2

Cunningham
Cres

Greendykes
Industrial
Estate

GREENDYKES B8020

Laing Gdns

Keith
Gdns

Pyothall Road

Clarkson Road

Nicol Road

Pyothall Road

McLeod St

Albyn
Park

Hoban
Sq

Hillview Avenue

alloway

Crescent

Erskine Rd

Pyothall Ct

Fergusson Rd

Sports
Centre

Stewartfield Road

Aitken Orr Drive

Hillview Pl

Broxburn
Academy

Globe Pk

McIntosh Ct

Nicol Pl

Buchan
Park

Albyn
Terr

Liggat
Pl

Curran Crescent

Mauden Rd

Kirkhill
Ct

Clarkson Road

Pyothall Ct

Bridge Place

Hanover
Ct

Shields
Ct

Primrose Ct

Stewartie Cres

Paterson's
Ct

Globe Pk

Union Road

Port Buchan

Holy-
gate
La

Buchan La

ROAD B8020

Rendall
Gdns

Blairmuir
Terr

scent

Globe
Park

Lumsden
Ct

Moore
Cotts

Kirkhill
Pl

Lychgate
Pl

School Rd

Buchan La

P.O

L

EAST

Church Road

Easter Rd

MAIN

Blyth

STREET

avenue

Kirkhill
Terr

Buchan Rd

Kirkhill
Rd

Kirkhill
Rd

Buchan
Ct

New
Holygate

W Burnside

Strath-
brock Pl

Argyle
Ct

Swim
Pool

Gordon
Ct

Melbourne Rd

Factory

AIN

STREET

Ashbank
Cotts

Parkwood Gdns

Brox Burn

Almondell Road

Webster
Ct

Almon-
dell Ct

Old Mill
Rd

Old Town

P

Power Station Rd

Bishops
Gate

Park Road

Alexander
Park

West Hall

Almondell Road

Linn
Pl

Grange Rd

A89

26

Woodville Ct

Parklands

Parkwood
Cres

Queens Road

St Johns Rd

Joseph Scott
Gdns

To Edinburgh

Brox Burn

St Nicholas
Primary

Badger Wk

Brook

Badger Moss

Parklands

Queens Ave

P

Broxburn

4

Badger
La

Blyth

Badger
Pl

Badger
Brook

Badger
Gro

eens Rd

A89

Badger
Park

dings

dger
ark

Holmes
Holdings

Ryal
Park

Ryal
Cotts

Ryal Burn

Park House

Caw Burn

Holmes
Cottages

Hawthorn
Brae

Powflats

Park House

Learielaw

5

Union Canal

To Glasgow
& Edinburgh

M8

E F G H

Index to street names can be found overleaf

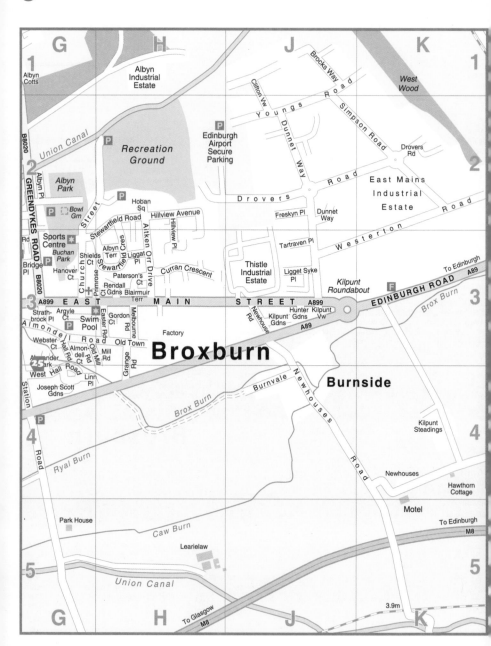

Broxburn

Burnside

x to Broxburn
ohall

Orr Drive	H3	East Main Street (Uphall)	C4	Joseph Scott Gardens	G4	Pentland View	C3
Cottages	G1, G2	East Main Street (Broxburn)	G3	Keith Gardens	E2	Port Buchan	F3
Place	G2	Ecclesmachan Road	B2	Kelso Street	D3	Power Station Road	E4
Terrace	H3	Edinburgh Road	K3	Kilpunt Gardens	J3	Primrose Court	H3
der Park	G3	Ellis Place	D3	Kilpunt Steadings	K4	Pyothall Court	F3
der Street	C4	Erskine Road	E2	Kilpunt View	J3	Pyothall Road	F2
dell Court	G3	Fairnsfell	D3	Kirkflat Avenue	C3	Queens Avenue	G4
dell Road	G3	Fergusson Road	G3	Kirkhill Court	E3	Queens Road	G4
Court	G3	Fernlea	B3	Kirkhill Park	E3	Rashierig	D3
nk Cottages	F3	Fivestanks Court	C3	Kirkhill Place	F3	Rendall Gardens	H3
r Brook	F4	Fivestanks Place	D3	Kirkhill Road	F3	Rosemount Drive	A4
r Court	E4	Forkneuk Road	A4	Kirkhill Terrace	E3	Ross's Walk	B4
r Grove	F4	Forkneuk Steadings	A4	Laing Gardens	E2	Ryal Cottages	F4
r Lane	E4	Forrest Walk	B4	Liggat Place	H3	St Andrews Court	B4
r Meadows	F4	Freeland Avenue	D3	Liggat Syke	D3	St Andrews Drive	A4
r Park	E4	Freeland Terrace	D3	Ligget Syke Place	J3	St John's Road	G4
r Place	E4	Freskyn Place	J2	Linn Place	G4	Saughbank	D3
r Walk	E4	Galloway Crescent	E2	Loanfoot Crescent	C3	School Place	B4
le Drive	B4	Galmeilon	E3	Loanfoot Road	C3	School Road	F3
os Gate	E3	Glebe Avenue	E3	Loaninghill Cottages	C4	Shambles, The	E4
uir Terrace	H3	Glebe Place	C4	Loaninghill Park	D4	Shields Court	G3
Road	E4	Glebe Road	C4	Loaninghill Road	D4	Simpson Road	K2
ensbrae	D3	Glebe Terrace	C3	Long Byres	G3	South Middleton	C5
Place	G3	Globe Park	E3	Lumsden Court	E3	Stankards Road	B5
s Way	J1	Gordon Court	H3	Lyarthall	D3	Station Road (Uphall)	B5
n Court	F3	Goschen Place	D3	Lychgate Lane	F3	Station Road (Broxburn)	G3
n Lane	G3	Goschen Terrace	D3	MacFarlane Place	B5	Stewartfield Crescent	H3
n Road	E3	Grange Road	H4	MacLardy Court	B5	Stewartfield Road	H2
de Road	C4	Greendykes Road	G2	McCann Avenue	D3	Strathbrock Place (Uphall)	B4
ale	J4	Greendykes Steadings	G1	McIntosh Court	E3	Strathbrock Place (Broxburn)	G3
ope Road	D4	Hall Road	G3	McLeod Street	G2	Tartraven Place	J3
oss Avenue	D3	Hanover Court	G3	Manse Park	B3	Thomson Court	B4
oss Crescent	E3	Hawthorn Place	B4	Mauldeth Road	E2	Thomson Grove	B4
oss Place	E3	Henderson Crescent	D3	Melbourne Road	H3	Timmeryetts	D2
oss Road	E3	Henderson Place	D3	Middleton Avenue	C4	Union Road	F3
dubs Avenue	C3	Hillview Avenue	H2	Middleton Road	C4	Webster Court	G3
dubs Crescent	C3	Hillview Place	H3	Mill Road	H3	West Burnside	G3
h Street	G3	Hoban Square	H2	Millbank Place	B4	Westerton Road	J3
on Road	E3, F2	Holmes Cottages	E5	Moore Cottages	F3	Westhall Gardens	C4
orn Drive	D3	Holmes Court	D4	Muirfield Drive	B4	West Hall Road	G4
View	J1	Holmes Farm Lane	D4	Muirs Court	B4	West Main Street (Uphall)	B4
ngar Avenue	C5	Holmes Holdings	D5, E4	New Holygate	F3	West Main Street (Broxburn)	E3
seaton	D2	Holmes Road	E4	Newhouses	K4	West Park Grove	D3
green Drive	C3	Holmes Smallholdings	E4	Newhouses Road	J4	West Holmes Place	D4
green Place	C3	Holygate Place	F3	Nicol Place	F3	West Holmes Road	D4
ngham	F2	Houston Gardens	B5	Nicol Road	F2	Whinrig	E2
cent		Howieson Green	B4	Old Mill Road	G3	Wilson Terrace	D3
Crescent	H3	Hunter Gardens	J3	Old Town	H3	Woodville Court	F4
Place	C3	Johnston Avenue	B5	Parklands	F4	Wyndford Avenue	C3
as Wynd	D2	Johnston Court	B4	Park Court	D3	Wyndford Place	C3
rs Road	J2	Joseph Cumming Gardens	D4	Park Road	G3	Youngs Road	J2
Street	D3			Park Terrace	D3		
et Way	J2			Parkview	D3		
r Road	H3			Parkwood Crescent	F4		
				Parkwood Gardens	F3		
				Patersons Court	H3		

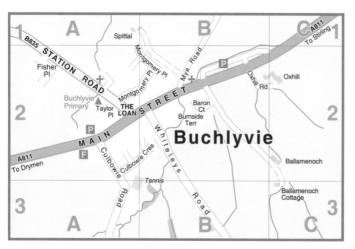

Buchlyvie

Index to Buchlyvie

Baron Court
Burnside Terrace
Culbowie Crescent
Culbowie Road
Fisher Place
Loan, The
Main Street
Montgomery Place
Mye Road
Oxhill Road
Station Road
Taylor Place
Whiteleys Road

Index to Callander

Achray Avenue
Ancaster Road
Ancaster Square

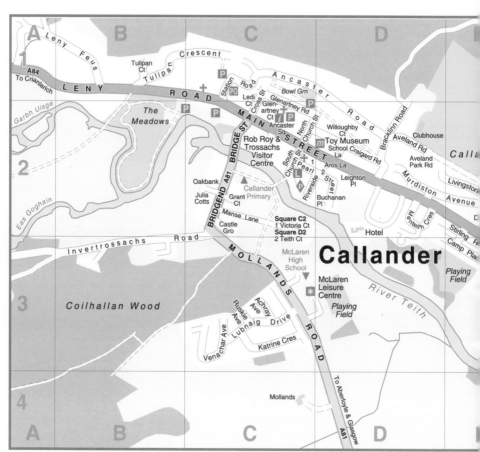

Callander

s Lane	D2	Grant Court	C2	Mollands Road	C3	Waverley Drive	E3
land Park Road	D2	Gullipen View	E3	Murdiston Avenue	D2	Willoughby Court	D2
land Road	D2	Invertrossachs Road	B3	North Church Street	C2	Willoughby Place	E3
gibbon Drive	E2	Julia Cottages	C2	Oakbank	C2		
cklinn Road	D2	Katrine Crescent	C3	Pearl Street	C2		
ge Street	C2	Lagrannoch Crescent	E3	Ritchie Place	E3		
gend	C2	Lagrannoch Drive	F3	Riverside	C2		
chanan Place	D2	Lagrannoch Way	F3	Robertson Way	F3		
np Place	E3	Ledi Court	C1	Ruskie Avenue	C1		
mpbell Court	E3	Leighton Place	D2	School Lane	D2		
tle Grove	C2	Lendrick Avenue	F3	South Church Street	C2		
igard Road	D2	Leny Feus	B1	Station Road	C1		
ss Street	C2	Leny Road	B1	Stirling Road	E3		
mmond Place	E2	Livingstone Avenue	E2	Teith Court (2)	D2		
er Crescent	E3	Lubnaig Drive	C3	Tulipan Court	B1		
glas Gardens	E3	McLaren Terrace	F3	Tulipan Crescent	B1		
sher Road	E3	Main Street	C2	Venachar Avenue	C3		
n Gardens	E2	Manse Lane	C2	Victoria Court (1)	D2		
nartney Court	C2	Marshall Crescent	E3	Vorlich Crescent	F3		
nartney Road	C2	Menteith Crescent	D2				
ngyle Place	F3						

Index to Cowie

Alloway Drive	B2
Ardgowan Place	C1
Armour Avenue	B2
Bannockburn Road	A2
Berryhill	B2
Brig o'Doon Grove	C2
Burns Terrace	B2
Carnock Street	C1
Cowiehall Road	B1
Dr Campbell Avenue	B1
Easterton Crescent	C2
Easterton Drive	C2
Easterton Grove	C2
Farm Road	B1
Fincastle Place	B1

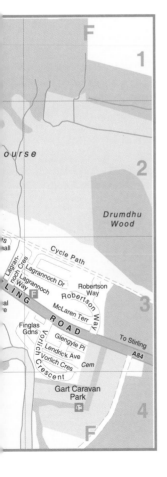

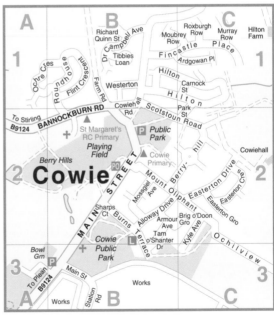

Index to Cowie

Flint Crescent	B1	Ochre Crescent	B1
Hilton	B1	Park Street	C2
Kyle Avenue	C2	Richard Quinn Street	B1
Main Street	B2, B3	Roundhouse	B1
Mossgiel Avenue	B2	Roxburgh Row	C1
Moubrey Row	B1	Scotstoun Road	B2
Mount Oliphant	B2	Sharps Court	B2
Murray Row	C1	Station Road	B3
Ochilview	C2	Tibbies Loan	B1
		Tam o'Shanter Drive	B2
		Westerton	B1

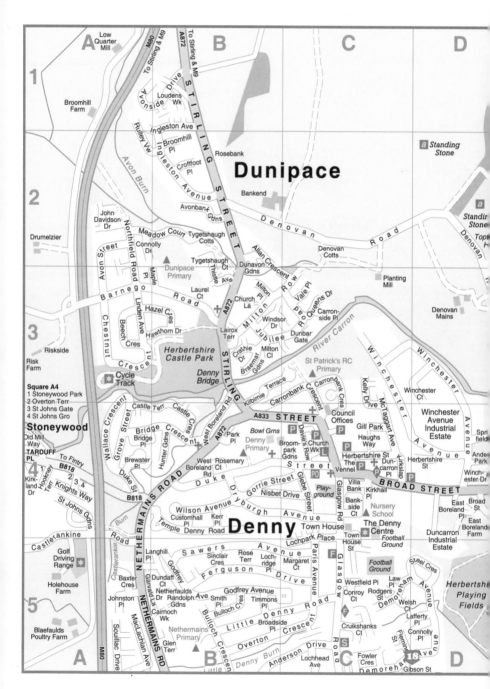

Low Quarter Mill
To Stirling & M9
To Stirling & M9
M80
A872
Broomhill Farm
Avonside Drive
Loudens Wk
Ingleston Ave
Broomhill Pl
Croftfoot Pl
Rulley Vw
Ingleston Avenue
STIRLING STREET
Rosebank

Dunipace

a Standing Stone

Bankend
Avonban Gdns
Denovan Road
Denovan Cotts
Planting Mill
a Standing Stone
Top H
Denovan

Drumelzier
John Davidson Dr
Avon Street
Northfield Road
Meadow Court
Connolly Dr
Tygetshaugh Cotts
Tygetshaugh Thistle Ct
Dunipace Primary
Alian Crescent
Dunavon Gdns
Row
Vale Pl
Denovan Mains

Barnego Road
Maple
Linden Ave
Hazel Cres
Laurel Ct
Church La
Milton Row
Peo Queens Dr
Carronside Pl

Chestnut
Beech Cres
Hawthorn Dr
Lairox Terr
Windsor Dr
Jubilee
Dunbar Gate
River Carron
Winchester

Riskside
Risk Farm
Crescent
Herbertshire Castle Park
Crathie Dr
Milton Cl
Braemar Gdns
St Patrick's RC Primary
Carronbank Cres
Kelly Drive
McTaggart Ave
Winchester Ct
Winchester Avenue

Cycle Track
Denny Bridge
STIRLING
Kilbirnie Terrace
Carronbank C Crescent
Winchester Avenue Industrial Estate
Spri field

Square A4
1 Stoneywood Park
2 Overton Terr
3 St Johns Gate
4 St Johns Gro

Stoneywood

Old Mill Way
TARDUFF PL
To Fintry
B818
Kirkland Dr
Hookney Terr
Knights Way
St Johns Gdns

Wallace Crescent
Castle Terr
Castle Crescent
Grove Street
Bridge Pl
Hunter Gdns
West Boreland Rd
A872
A833 STREET
Bowl Grns
Park Pl
Denny Primary
Broompark Gdns
Church Wk
Haughs Way
Gill Park
Council Offices
Herbertshire St
Herbertshire St
Ande Park

Brewster Pl
Duke St
West Rosemary Boreland Ct
Duke Street
Gorrie Street
Glebe Street
The Vennel
Dun-carron Pl
Winchester Dr

B818
Dryburgh Avenue
Nisbet Drive
Playground
Villa Bank
Kirkhall Pl
PO
BROAD STREET
East Boreland Pl
Broad St
East Boreland Farm

Customhall Pl
Kerr Pl
Denny Road
Wilson Avenue
Town House
Bankside Ct
Nursery School
The Denny Centre
Duncarron Industrial Estate

Castletankine
Golf Driving Range
Temple Road
Langhill Pl
Sawers Avenue
Sinclair Cres
Rose Terr
Lochridge
Margaret Ct
Lochpark Place
Town House St
Football Ground
Glasgow Rd

Denny

Holehouse Farm
Baxter Cres
Dundaff Ct
Godfrey
Ferguson Pl
Paris Avenue
Drive
Football Ground
Westfield Pl
Conroy Ct
Law Pl
Rodgers St
Steel Cres
Herbertshi Playing Fields

Blaefaulds Poultry Farm
MacLachlan Ave
NETHERMAINS RD
Johnston Pl
Netherfaulds Dr
Randolph Ave
Smith Gdns
Godfrey Avenue
Timmons
Welsh Ct
Lafferty Pl
Connolly Pl

M80
Souillac Drive
Cairnoch Wk
Bulloch Cres
Nethermains Primary
Glen Terr
Little Denny Road
Broadside Pl
Overton Crescent
Cruikshanks Ct
Fleming
Anderson Drive
Lochhead Ave
Fowler Cres
Gibson St
18

Denny Burn
Anderson Drive
Demoreh

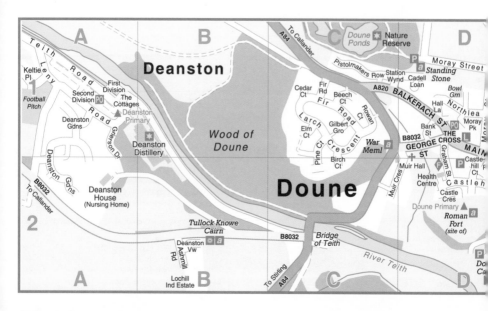

Index to Doune & Deanston

Ardochbank	E2	Graham Street	D1
Ashmill Road	B2	Grierson Drive	A1
Balkerach Street	D1	Hall Lane	D1
Bank Street	D1	Inverardoch Cottages	E2
Beech Court	C1	Keltie Place	A1
Birch Court	C1	King Street	D1
Cadell Loan	D1	Larch Crescent	C1
Castle Crescent	D2	Leny Road	A1
Castle Road	D2	Main Street	D1
Castlehill Court	D2	Moray Park	D1
Castlehill	D2	Moray Street	D1
Cedar Court	C1	Muir Crescent	C2
Cottages, The	A1	Northlea	D1
Cross, The	D1	Park Lane	D2
Deanston Gardens	A1	Pine Court	C1
Deanston View	B2	Pistolmakers Row	C1
Elm Court	C1	Queen Street	D2
Fir Road	C1	Rowan Court	C1
First Division	A1	Second Division	A1
George Street	D1	Station Wynd	C1
Gilbert Grove	C1	Teith Road	A1

Index to Drymen

Ardmore Gardens	C2
Ballyconachy Loan	A2
Balmaha Road	B2
Castle Gardens	A2
Charles Crescent	C2
Clairinch Way	B2
Conic Way	B2
Credon Way	B2
Gartness Court	C3
Gartness Road	C2, E5
Main Street	B3
Montrose Way	B2
Muirpark Way	B2
Old Balmaha Road	B2
Old Gartmore Road	B2
Old Military Road	A5, C2
Square, The	B2
Stirling Road	C2
Stuart Drive	C2
Winnock Court	B2

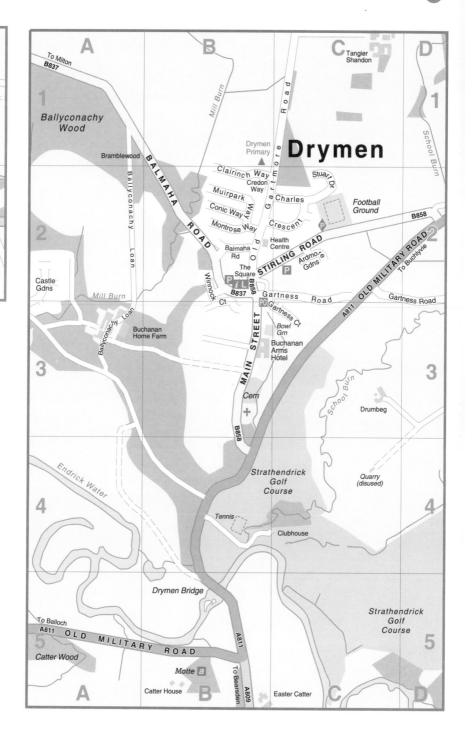

Drymen

Ballyconachy Wood

To Milton
B837

Bramblewood

BALMAHA ROAD

Ballyconachy Loan

Mill Burn

Castle Gdns

Ballyconachy Loan

Buchanan Home Farm

Winnock Ct

MAIN STREET

Drymen Primary

Clairinch Way
Credon Way
Muirpark Way
Conic Way
Montrose Way

Gartmore Road

Stuart Dr
Charles Crescent

Old Stirling Road

Balmaha Rd

The Square

P i L
B837 B858

Gartness Road

PO Gartness Ct

Bowl Grn

Buchanan Arms Hotel

Cem

B858

Endrick Water

Drymen Bridge

To Balloch
A811 OLD MILITARY ROAD

Catter Wood

Motte a

Catter House

A811

To Bearsden

A809

Easter Catter

Tangier Shandon

Football Ground

B858

A811 OLD MILITARY ROAD

To Buchlyvie

Gartness Road

School Burn

Health Centre

Ardmore Gdns

P

School Burn

Drumbeg

Quarry (disused)

Strathendrick Golf Course

Tennis

Clubhouse

Strathendrick Golf Course

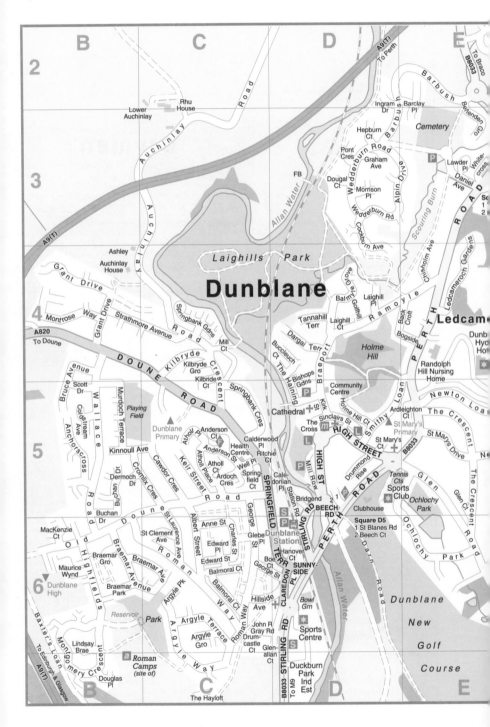

DUNBLANE

B C D E

2

To Braco
B8033

Barbush
A9(T)
To Perth

Rhu House
Lower Auchinlay

Ingram Dr Barclay Pl
Hepburn Ct **Cemetery**

3

Auchinlay
FB
Allan Water

Pont Cres
Dougal Ct
Morrison Pl
Graham Ave
Wedderburn Road
Wedderburn Rd
Cockburn Ave

P
Lawder Pl White-cross
Daniel Ave
ROAD
So
1
2

Ashley
Auchinlay House

Laighills Park

Scouring Burn
Chisholm Ct
Ledcameroch Gardens

D

Grant Drive

Dunblane

Balmy Goldhill
Laighill Pl
Tannahill Terr Laighill Terr
Laighill Ct
Ramoyle
Back Croft
Bogside
PERTH

Ledcam

Dunb Hyd Hot

4

Montrose Way Grant Drive
Strathmore Avenue
A820
To Doune

Springbank Gdns
Road
Mill Ct

Dargai Terr
Buccleuch Ct
The Haining
Bishops Gdns

Holme Hill
Randolph Hill Nursing Home

Newton Loa

DOUNE ROAD

Kilbryde Gro
Kilbride Ct
Springbank Cres

P
Community Centre
Home Hill Ct
Kirk St
Ardleighton Ct
St Mary's Primary
The Crescent
St Marys Drive

5

Bruce Avenue
Scott Dr
Cowdream Ave
Murdoch Terrace
Playing Field
Kinnoull Ave
Anchorscross
Dermoch Dr
Cromlix Cres
Buchan Dr

Dunblane Primary
Anderson Ct
Atholl Pl
Anderson Ct
Cawdor Cres
Keir Street
Atholl Ct
Ardoch Cres
Road
Calderwood Pl
Ritchie Ct
Health Centre
Well Pl
Springfield Ct

SPRINGFIELD
Caledonian Pl
Mill Row
Station Rd

Cathedral Kirk
The Cross Sinclairs St
St Mary's Ct
B8033
HIGH STREET
L Smithy
Drummond Rise
Tennis Cts
Sports Club
Ochlochy Park
Glen Ct
The Crescent

Glen
Ochlochy Park

6

MacKenzie Ct
Old Highfields
Braemar Gro
Maurice Wynd
Braemar Park
Dunblane High
Baxter's Loan
To Edinburgh & Glasgow
A9(T)

St Clement Ave
Albert Street
Roman
St Laurence Ave
Anne St
Charles St
Edward Pl
Edward St
Balmoral Ct
George St
Glebe St
George St
Boe...
Dunblane Station
Hanover Ct
Hillside Ave
John R Gray Rd
Drumcastle Ct
Glenallan Ct

SPRINGFIELD TERR
Bridgend
Glebe Pl
CLAREDON PL
STIRLING RD
SUNNY-SIDE

Bridgend
BEECH RD
Clubhouse
PERTH ROAD

Square D5
1 St Blanes Rd
2 Beech Ct

Bowl Grn
Sports Centre

Allan Water
Darn Road

Dunblane
New
Golf
Course

Lindsay Brae
Montgomery Crescent
Douglas Pl

Reservoir Park
Roman Camps (site of)

Argyle Pk
Argyle Terrace
Argyle Gro
Argyle Way

B8033 STIRLING RD
To M9

Duckburn Park Ind Est

B C D E

The Hayloft

Index to Dunblane

Street	Grid	Street	Grid	Street	Grid
Albert Street	C6	Edward Place	C6	Old Doune Road	B6
Alpin Drive	D3	Edward Street	C6	Perth Road	D6
Anchorscross	B5	George Street	C6	Pont Crescent	D3
Anderson Court	C5	Gibson Grove	E6	Ramoyle	D4
Anderson Street	C5	Glebe Place	C6	Ramsay Drive	F3
Anne Street	C6	Glen Court	E5	Ritchie Court	C5
Ardleighton Court	E5	Glen Road	E5, F6	Robertson Road	F4
Ardnablane	F5	Glenallan Court	D6	Roman Way	C6
Ardoch Crescent	C5	Golfhill	D4	Rylands Avenue	F3
Argyle Grove	C6	Graham Avenue	D3	Rylands Road	F3
Argyle Park	C6	Grant Drive	B4	St Blanes Road (1)	D5
Argyle Terrace	C6	Haining, The	D5	St Clement Avenue	C6
Argyle Way	C6	Hanover Court	D6	St Laurence Avenue	C6
Atholl Court	C5	Hayloft, The	C7	St Margarets Drive	E5
Atholl Place	C5	Hepburn Court	D3	St Margarets Loan	E5
Auchinlay Road	C3	High Street	D5	St Mary's Court	D5
Back Croft	E4	Highfields	B6	St Marys Drive	E5
Balmoral Court	C6	Hillside Avenue	C6	Scott Drive	B5
Balmyle Grove	D4	Holme Hill Court	D5	Sheriffmuir Road	F7
Barbush	D3	Ingram Drive	D2	Sinclairs Street	D5
Barbush	E2	John R Gray Road	C6	Smithy Loan	D5
Barclay Place	E3	Keir Street	C5	Springbank Crescent	C5
Baxter's Loan	B6	Kellie Wynd	F3, F4	Springbank Gardens	C4
Beech Court (2)	D5	Kilbride Court	C4	Springfield Court	C5
Beech Road	D5	Kilbryde Crescent	C4	Springfield Terrace	C5
Bellenden Grove	E2	Kilbryde Grove	C4	Station Road	D5
Bishops Gardens	D4	King Edward Walk	E2	Stirling Road	D6, D7
Boe Court	C6	Kinnoull Avenue	B5	Strathmore Avenue	B4
Bogside	E4	Kippendavie Avenue	E3	Sunnyside	D6
Braemar Avenue	B6	Kippendavie Lane	F3	Symon Field	F5
Braemar Grove	B6	Kippendavie Mains	F3	Tannahill Terrace	D4
Braemar Park	B6	Kippendavie Road	E3	Wallace Road	B5
Braeport	D4	Kirk Street	D5	Wedderburn Road	D3
Bridgend	D5	Laighill Court	D4	Well Place	C5
Bruce Avenue	B5	Laighill Place	D4	Whitecross Avenue	E3
Bruce Brae	E3	Landrick Avenue (2)	E3		
Buccleuch Court	D4	Landrick Terrace (1)	E3		
Buchan Drive	B5	Lawder Place	E3		
Calderwood Place	C5	Ledcameroch Gardens	E4		
Caledonian Place	D5	Leewood Park	F6		
Cawdor Crescent	C5	Leewood Road	E6		
Charles Street	C6	Leighton Avenue	F5		
Chisholm Avenue	E4	Leighton Court	F5		
Claredon Place	D6	Lindsay Brae	B6		
Cockburn Avenue	D3	MacKenzie Court	B6		
Coldstream Avenue	B5	Maurice Wynd	B6		
Crescent, The	E5	Menteith View	F4		
Cromlix Crescent	B5	Mill Court	C4		
Cross, The	D5	Mill Row	D5		
Daniel Avenue	E3	Montgomery Crescent	B6		
Dargai Terrace	D4	Montrose Way	B4		
Darn Road	D6	Morrison Place	D3		
Dermoch Drive	B5	Murdoch Terrace	B5		
Dougal Court	D3	Nason Avenue	E2		
Douglas Place	B7	Newton Crescent	F4		
Doune Road	C5	Newton Loan	E5		
Drumcastle Court	C6	Ochiltree Court	F5		
Drummond Rise	D5	Ochiltree	E4		
Dykedale	F5	Ochlochy Park	E6		

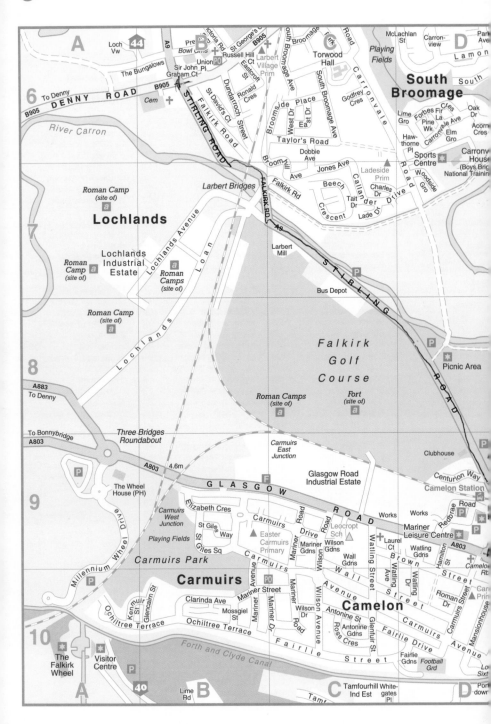

Loch Vw
44
A9

Pre
Bowl Gdns
Victoria Rd
St George's Ct
B505

McLachlan St
Carron-view
Park Ave
Lamon

A

B

C

D

Russell Hill Ct
Larbert Village Prim
Torwood Hall

Playing Fields

South Broomage
South

Union
20
Sir John Pl
Graham Ct
St John Pl
St David's Ct
Dundarroch Street
Ronald Cres
Eastcroft
Broomside Place
West Dr
Ear St
South Broomage Ave
South Broomage Ave
Godfrey Cres
Lime Gro
Forbes Fir Ctes
Pine La
Wk
Oak Dr
Acorn Cres

6
To Denny
B905
DENNY ROAD
B905
Cem

St Davids Ct
Taylor's Road
Dobbie Ave
Hawthorne Pl
Carronvale Ave
Elm Gro

River Carron

Broom Mill
Ave
Jones Ave
Ladeside Prim
Sports Centre
Woodside Gro
Carrony House
(Boys Bric National Traini

Roman Camp
(site of)
a
Lochlands
Larbert Bridges
Falkirk Road
Stirling Road
Falkirk Rd
Falkirk Rd
Beech
Callander Drive
Charles Dr
Lade Dr
A9

7
Roman Camp
(site of)
a
Lochlands Industrial Estate
Lochlands Avenue
Roman Camps
(site of)
a
Lochlands Loan
Tait Dr
Crescent
Larbert Mill
STIRLING

Roman Camp
(site of)
a
Bus Depot

8
A883
To Denny

*Falkirk
Golf
Course*

Roman Camps
(site of)
a
Fort
(site of)
a
ROAD
P
Picnic Area

To Bonnybridge
A803
Three Bridges Roundabout
A803
4.6m
Carmuirs East Junction
Clubhouse
Centurion Way
Camelon Station

9
P
The Wheel House (PH)
Millennium Wheel Drive
Carmuirs West Junction
Playing Fields
Elizabeth Cres
St Giles Way
St Gile Sq
GLASGOW ROAD
Carmuirs
Mariner Road
Wilson Road
Glasgow Road Industrial Estate
Works
Leocropt Sch
Wilson Gdns
Mariner Gdns
Works
Wall Gdns
Laurel Ct
Mariner Leisure Centre
Watling Gdns
Redbrae Road
P
A803

Carmuirs Park
Carmuirs
Kennuir St
Glencairn St
Clarinda Ave
Mossgiel St
Mariner Street
Mariner Avenue
Mariner Dr
Carmuirs
Mariner Road
Wilson Dr
Wall Avenue
Antonine St
Antonine Gdns
Ross Cres
Watling Street
Watling Ave
Watling Dr
Brown Street
Hamilton St
Camelon
Fairlie Drive
Roman Dr
Carmuirs Avenue
Mansionhouse Road
Camelon
Rd
Cari
Prin

10
P
The Falkirk Wheel
Visitor Centre
P
40
Ochiltree Terrace
Ochiltree Terrace
Forth and Clyde Canal
Fairlie Street
Glenfuir St
Fairlie Gdns
Football Grd
Lo
Sixt
Po
down

A
B
Lime Rd
C
Tamfourhill White-gates Pl
Tamf
Ind Est
D

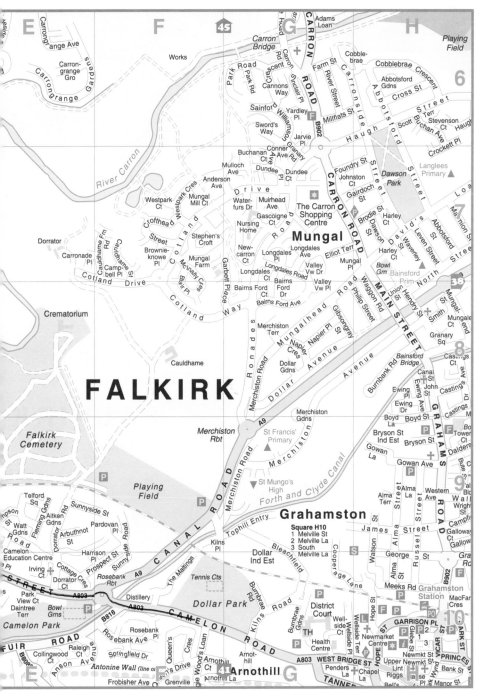

FALKIRK

Mungal

Grahamston

Falkirk Cemetery

Camelon Park

Playing Field (E6)

Playing Field

Crematorium

Cauldhame

The Carron Shopping Centre

Langlees Primary

Dawson Park

Bainsford Prim

Merchiston Rbt

St Francis' Primary

St Mungo's High

Forth and Clyde Canal

Square H10
1 Melville St
2 Melville La
3 South Melville La

Dollar Ind Est

Dollar Park

District Court

Grahamston Station

Health Centre

Newmarket Centre

GARRISON PL

Carrongrange Ave
Carrongrange Gro
Carrongrange Gardens
River Carron
Carron Bridge
Works
Park Road
Park Rd
Crescent Rd
Carron Sinclair Rd
Cannons Way
Sainford
Yardley Pl
Williamson
Sword's Way
Jarvie Pl
Granary
Conner Ave Rd
Buchanan Ct
Mulloch Ave
Anderson Ave
Dundee Ct
Dundee
Westpark Ct
Mungal Mill Ct
Crofthead
Stephen's Croft
Street
Brownie-knowe Pl
Mungal Farm
Water-furs Dr
Muirhead Ave
Gascoigne Ct
Nursing Home
New-carron Rd
Longdales Pl
Longdales Ave
Longdales Road
Longdales Ct
Bairns Ford Ct
Bairns Ford Dr
Bairns Ford Ave
Valley Vw Dr
Valley Vw Pl
Elliot Terr
Mungal Pl
Bowl Grn
Dorrator
Carronade Pl
Cauldhame Fm Rd
Campbell Pl
Cauldhame St
McAnally Cres
Mungal Pl
Blair Pl
Cotland Drive
Cotland
Garbett Place
Cotland Way
Ronades
Merchiston Terr
Merchiston Road
Mungalhead Rd
Napier Cres
Napier Pl
Gibsongray
Dollar Gdns
Dollar Avenue
Avenue
Merchiston Gdns
A9
Canal Road
Merchiston Road
Merchiston
Telford Sq
Sunnyside St
Watt Gdns
Aitken Gdns
Fleming Gdns
Arbuthnot St
Pardovan Pl
Dorrator Rd
Sunny Road
Prospect St
Harrison St
Camelon Education Centre
Irving Ct
Cottage Cres
Dorrator Ct
Rosebank Rbt
Park View Ct
Daintree Terr
Bowl Grns
Distillery
Camelon Park
FUIR STREET
Collingwood Ct
Anson Ave
Raleigh Ct
Rosebank
Rosebank Ave
Springfield Dr
Queen's Cres
Wood's Loan
Antonine Wall (line of)
Frobisher Ave
Grenville
Arnothill Ct
Arnothill La
Arnothill
A803
CAMELON ROAD
B816
The Maltings
Kilns Pl
Tophill Entry
Tennis Cts
Bleachfield
Cooperage Lane
Bumbrae Road
Kilns Road
Burnbrae Gdns
TH
Wellside La
Wellside Terr
James Street
Alma Terr
Alma La
Alma Street
Alma St
George St
Russel St
Western Ave
Wright
Watson
Hope St
Meeks Rd
WEST BRIDGE ST
A803
Penders La
Chapel La
Upper Newmkt
Lint Riggs
Newmkt St
VICAR ST
HOPE
Bank St
PRINCES
ARK ST
PARK ST
Manor St
TANNER
ARNOTHILL

CARRON ROAD
MAIN STREET
RIVER STREET
CARRONSIDE
HAUGH
Abbotsford Gdns
Cross St
Abbotsford Street
Scott St
Buchan Ave
Stevenson Terr
Crockett Pl
Abbotsford Street
Foundry St
Johnston Ct
Gairdoch St
Brodie Ct
Dawson St
Harley Ct
Harley Ct
David's Loan
Leven Street
Waverley Street
North
Mungalend
Granary Sq
Castings Ct
Waggon Rd
Philip Street
Union Rd
Hendry St
Smith St
Mungal Ct
Bainsford Bridge
Canal St
John St
Ewing Pl
Ewing Dr
Boyd St
Boyd La
Boyd St
Bryson St
Ind Est
Bryson St
Gowan La
Gowan Ave
GRAHAMS ROAD
Castings
Tower Ct
Dalders
Bute
Campfi
Galloway Ct
Gallow
Gra Rd
B902
MacFarlane Cres
Wynd
Bell's

Cobblebrae
Cobblebrae Crescent
Farm St
Adams Loan
B902
Millflatts St

Index to street names can be found overleaf

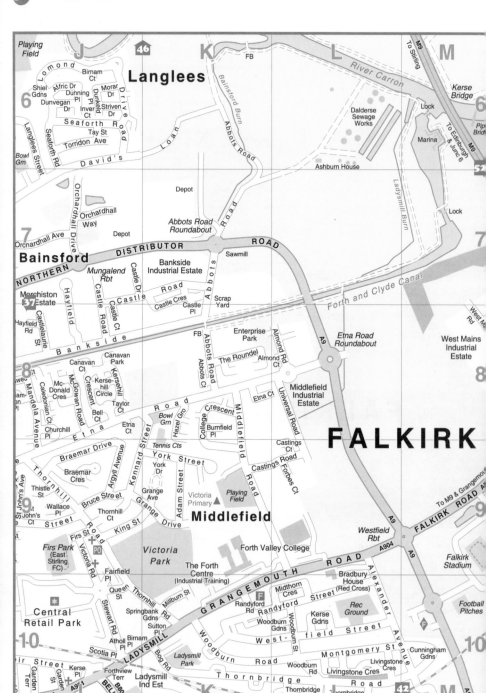

J **46** **K** FB **L** To Stirling M9 **M**

Playing Field

Lomond
Birnam Ct
Shiel Gdns
Afric Dr
Dunning Pl
Dunkeld Dr
Morar Dr
Dunvegan Dr
Inver Ct
Striven Dr
Langlees

Kerse Bridge

To Edinburgh & Junc 6
Lock

6

Seaforth Road
Tay St
Torridon Ave
Seaforth Rd
Langlees Street
David's

Bainsford Burn

Abbots Road
River Carron
Dalderse Sewage Works

Marina

Pip Brid
M9

Bowl Grn

Orchardhall Drive
Orchardhall Way
Orchardhall Ave
Depot
Depot

Abbots Road Roundabout

Abbots Road

Ashburn House

Ladysmill Burn
Lock

7

Bainsford
NORTHERN
DISTRIBUTOR
ROAD
Sawmill

Forth and Clyde Canal

7

Morchiston Estate **37**
Mungalend Rbt
Hayfield
Castle Dr
Castle Rd
Castle Ct
Castle Road
Castle
Road
Castle Cres
Castle Pl
Scrap Yard
Bankside Industrial Estate
Abbots

West Main Rd

Hayfield Rd
Castlelaurie St
Bankside
FB
Abbots Ct
Abbots Road
Enterprise Park
The Roundel
Almond Rd Ct
Almond Rd
Etna Road Roundabout
A9
West Mains Industrial Estate

8

Canavan Ct
Canavan Park
Kersehill Circle
Kersehill Crescent
McGowan Road
Caledonian Ct
Mc-Donald Cres
Mandela Avenue
Churchill Pl
Etna
Bell Ct
Taylor Ct
Etna Ct
Road
Bowl Grn
Hazel Gro
College Crescent
Burnfield Pl
Etna Ct
Middlefield Road
Universal Road
Middlefield Industrial Estate
Castings Ct
Castings Road
Forbes Ct

FALKIRK

8

Braemar Drive
Braemar Cres
Thornhill
Thistle St
Wallace Pl
Bruce Street
Argyll Avenue
Kennard Street
Tennis Cts
York Street
York Dr
Grange Ave
Adam Street
Victoria Primary
Playing Field

To M9 & Grangemouth
FALKIRK ROAD

9

St John's Ave
St John's Ct
Street
Thornhill Ct
Grange Drive
Middlefield

Falkirk Stadium

9

Firs Park (East Stirling FC)
Firs St
Victoria Rd
King St
Fairfield Pl
Queen St
Thornhill Rd
Millburn Rd
Victoria Park
The Forth Centre (Industrial Training)
Forth Valley College
GRANGEMOUTH ROAD A904
Westfield Rbt
Bradbury House (Red Cross)
Midthorn Cres
Randyford Rd
Randyford St
Rec Ground
Alexander Avenue
A9
Football Pitches

Central Retail Park
Springbank Gdns
Sutton Pl
Atholl Pl
Birnam Pl
Stewart Rd
West-field Street
Woodburn Gdns
Woodburn St
Kerse Gdns
Montgomery St
Cunningham Gdns

10

Scotia Pl
LADYSMILL
Bog Rd
Woodburn Road
Woodburn Rd
Livingstone Cres
Livingstone Cres
10

Street
Garden Terr
Kerse Garden
A9
Forthview Terr
BELLSM
B8080
Ladysmill Ind Est
Ladysmill Park
Thornbridge
Road
Thornbridge Sq
Thornbridge Gdns
42
A9

KERSE LA
J
K
M

ex to Falkirk, Larbert & Stenhousemuir

ts Court	K8	Baxter's Wynd	H11	Burnside Terrace	E10	Church Street	E5
ts Moss Drive	F14	Bean Row	H11	Bute Street	H9	(Stenhousemuir)	
ts Road	K7	Beaufort Drive	G4	Cadell Drive	G2	Church Street	J5
tsford Gardens	H6	Beauly Court	J14	Calder Place	K14	(Carronshore)	
tsford Street	H6	Beaumont Drive	G5	Caledonian Court	J8	Churchill Place	J8
crombie Street	E9	Beaumont Drive	H5	Callander Drive	C7	Clanranald Place	F13
ay Drive	F14	Beech Crescent	C7	Callendar Avenue	H14	Clarinda Avenue	B10
n Crescent	D6	Begg Avenue	E11	Callendar Boulevard	L11	Clarinda Place	C3
n Crescent	F5	Bell Court	J8	Callendar Park Drive	K11	Cluny Drive	F3
n Grossert Court	D4	Bell's Wynd	H10	Callendar Park View	K11	Clyde Crescent	B4
n Street	K9	Bellsdyke Place	A4	Callendar Park Walk	K11	Clyde Street	E10
ns Loan	G6	Bellsdyke Road	B4, L1	Callendar Riggs	J11	Cobblebrae Crescent	H6
c Drive	J6	Bellsmeadow Road	J10	Callendar Road	K11	Cobblebrae	H6
rey Drive	F3	Bellvue Street	J11	Cambus Avenue	C2	Cochrane Avenue	H11
ison Drive	B4	Belmont Street	J11	Camelon Road	F10	Cochrane Street	H11
ison Place	H10	Belmont Tower	J11	Cameron Place	H5	Cockburn Street	G11
n Gardens	E9	Birnam Court	J6	Campbell Drive	B5	College Crescent	K8
n Road	E9	Birnam Place	J10	Campbell Place	F7	Collingwood Court	E10
n Terrace	E9	Blackmill Crescent	H4	Campfield Street	H9	Colonsay Terrace	H13
it Road	F5	Blair Place	F7	Canal Road	F10	Comely Park Gardens	H11
rt Road	G12	Blair Terrace	G3	Canal Street	H8	Comely Park Terrace	H11
ander Avenue	L10	Blairdenon Crescent	F12	Canavan Court	J8	Comely Place	H11
bank Road	C5	Bleachfield	G9	Canavan Park	J8	Conner Avenue	G7
Barr Court	H14	Blenheim Place	E2	Canmore Drive	E3	Conway Court	F11
a Road	F3, G4, G5	Blinkbonny Road	E11	Cannons Way	G6	Cooperage Lane	G9
vay Wynd	C3	Bluebell Close (6)	H11	Carbrook Terrace	C4	Corentin Court	J12
a Lane	H9	Bog Road (Falkirk)	K10	Carmuirs Avenue	C10	Corporation Street	J11
a Street	H9	Bog Road (Lauriston)	M11	Carmuirs Drive	C9	Corrie Avenue	F3
a Terrace	H9	Bogend Road	C1	Carmuirs Street	D10	Corrie Place	D11
ond Court	L8	Booth Place	H11	Carnegie Drive	D9	Cortachy Avenue	G4
ond Road	L8	Bothkennar Road	K4	Carradale Avenue	C11	Cotland Drive	E7, F7
erson Avenue	F7	Boyd Lane	H9	Carrick Place (Tamfourhill)	C11	Cotland Way	F8
erson Drive	H5	Boyd Street	H9	Carrick Place (Carron)	G4	Cottage Crescent	E10
aster Place	G14	Bracken Avenue	G13	Carron Road	G7	Cottages, The	K14
ew Crescent	D3	Bracklinn Place	F14	Carronade Place	E7	Cow Wynd	H11, H12
an Court	J13	Bradbury Street	H5	Carronbank Avenue	H5	Craigairn Court	G13
e Drive	E3	Braemar Crescent	J9	Carronbank Court	H5	Craighorn Drive	E12
on Avenue	E11	Braemar Drive	J9	Carrongrange Avenue	E5	Craigie Court	B4
nine Gardens	C10	Braemar Place	G4	Carrongrange Gardens	E6	Craigievar Avenue	G4
nine Street	C10	Braeview (Larbert)	D6	Carrongrange Grove	E6	Craigleith Avenue	E12
thnot Street	E9	Braeview (Lauriston)	M12	Carrongrange Road	E5	Craigmillar Place	F3
reck Place	G4	Breton Court	J12	Carrongrove Avenue	G5	Cramond Court	H13
ll Avenue	J9	Brodick Place	C11	Carrongrove Road	G5	Crathes Avenue	G3
our Mews	B3	Brodie Street	H7	Carronhall Avenue	J3	Crawhall Place	B5
t Street	J11	Bronte Place	G4	Carronlea Drive	G5	Creteil Court	J11
thill Bank	G11	Broom Crescent	G13	Carronshore Road	H5	Crockett Place	H7
thill Court	F10	Broomage Avenue	B4	Carronside Street	G6	Crofthead Street	F7
thill Gardens	G11	Broomage Bank	C5	Carronvale Avenue	D6	Cromwell Drive	K11
thill Lane	F10	Broomage Crescent	B4	Carronvale Road	C6	Cromwell Road	K11
thill Mews	G11	Broomage Drive	B4	Carronview	D5	Cromwell Road West	K11
thill	G11	Broomage Park	C6	Castings Avenue	H8	Cross Street	H6
n Terrace	C11	Broomhill Avenue	C6	Castings Court (Middlefield)	L9	Crownest Loan	E5
ur's Drive	F5	Broomside Place	C6	Castings Court (Mungal)	H8	Cruachan Court	J13
Grove	F4	Brosdale Court	H13	Castings Drive	H8	Cuillin Court	J14
ll Place	J10	Brown Street	D9	Castings Road	K9	Culmore Place	L14
entyre Place	J4	Brownieknowe Place	F7	Castle Place	K7	Culvain Place	J13
Drive	M12	Bruart Avenue	F4	Castle Avenue	J4	Culzean Place	F3
ue, The	J5	Bruce Crescent	H4	Castle Court	J7	Cumbrae Drive	C11
Court	J13	Bruce Drive	F4	Castle Crescent	K7	Cunningham Gardens	M10
d Street	D10	Bruce Street	J9	Castle Drive (Carron)	G5	Cunningham Road	F4
ns Ford Avenue	G8	Bryce Avenue	H5	Castle Drive (Middlefield)	J7	Cursiter Court	B5
ns Ford Court	G8	Bryson Place	B2	Castle Road	J7	Cuttyfield Place	J4
ns Ford Drive	G8	Bryson Street	H9	Castlelaurie Street	J8	Daintree Terrace	E10
our Crescent	C5	Buchan Avenue	H6	Cauldhame Farm Road	F7	Dalderse Avenue	H9
noral Drive	E11	Buchanan Court	G7	Cauldhame Street	F7	Davarr Place	C11
noral Place	E3	Bungalows, The	B6	Cedar Grove	E6	David's Loan	H7
noral Street	E12	Burder Park	G5	Central Boulevard	B3	Dawson Street	H7
k Street	H10	Burnbank Road	H8	Central Drive	F4	Derwent Avenue	F11
kside	J8	Burnbrae Gardens	G10	Central Park Avenue	B3	Dobbie Avenue	C6
taskine Drive	F11	Burnbrae Road	G10	Centurion Way	D9	Dochart Place	K13
taskine Gardens	E11	Burnfield Place	K8	Chambers Drive	H5	Dock Street	J5
taskine Road	F11	Burnfoot Lane	G11	Chapel Crescent	H4	Dollar Avenue	G8
taskine Street	E12	Burnhead Lane	J11	Chapel Drive	E4	Dollar Gardens	G8
kin Court	H13	Burnhead Road	C4	Chapel Lane	H10	Dorrator Court	E10
nton Lane (8)	H11	Burns Avenue	C2	Charles Drive	C7	Dorrator Road	E9
ra Place	G3	Burns Crescent	M11	Charlotte Hill Court	B4	Douglas Place	F3
rie Road	F4	Burnside Place	H4	Chestnut Grove	F4	Doune Crescent	G3
				Christie Terrace	F4	Dow Lane	G4
				Church Place	H9	Dow Place	G4

Index to street names is continued on page 43

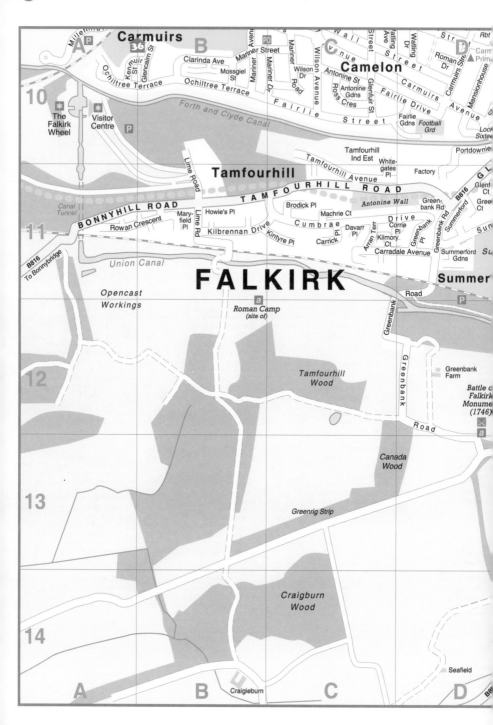

Carmuirs

36

Clarinda Ave

Mossgiel St

Kennuir St

Glencairn St

Ochiltree Terrace

Ochiltree Terrace

Mariner Avenue

Mariner Street

Mariner Dr

Mariner Road

Wilson Dr

Wilson Avenue

PO

C

Camelon

Antonine St

Antonine Gdns

Ross Cres

Glenfuir St

Watling Street

Street

Watling Dr

Wall

Roman Site

Roman Dr

Str

D

Rbt

Carm Prim

Mansionhouse

Carmuirs

Fairlie Drive

Carmuirs Avenue

Fairlie Gdns

Football Grd

Loch Sixtee

Portdownie

GL

10

The Falkirk Wheel

Visitor Centre

P

Forth and Clyde Canal

Street

Fairlie Street

Tamfourhill

Lime Road

Tamfourhill Avenue

Tamfourhill Ind Est

White-gates Pl

Factory

B816

Glenf Ct

Gree Ct

Canal Tunnel

BONNYHILL ROAD

Rowan Crescent

Mary-field Pl

Lime Rd

Howie's Pl

Kilbrennan Drive

TAMFOURHILL ROAD

Brodick Pl

Machrie Ct

Cumbrae

Carrick

Kintyre Pi

Davarr Pl

Arran Terr

Antonine Wall

Drive

Corrie Pl

Kilmory Ct

Carradale Avenue

Greenbank Pl

Greenbank Rd

Green-bank Rd

Summerford

Summerford Gdns

Sun

Su

11

B816
To Bonnybridge

Union Canal

FALKIRK

Opencast Workings

Roman Camp
(site of)

a

Road

P

Summer

Greenbank

12

Tamfourhill Wood

Greenbank

Road

Greenbank Farm

Battle c Falkirk Monume (1746)

a

Canada Wood

13

Greenrig Strip

Craigburn Wood

14

Seafield

A

B

Craigieburn

C

Craigieburn

D

Be

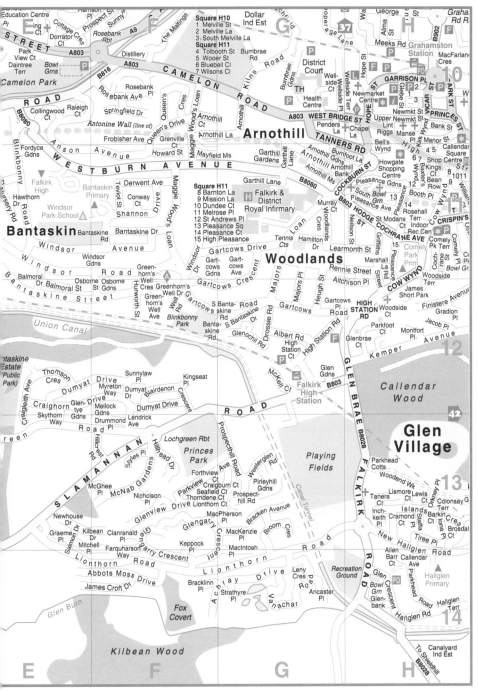

Index to street names can be found overleaf

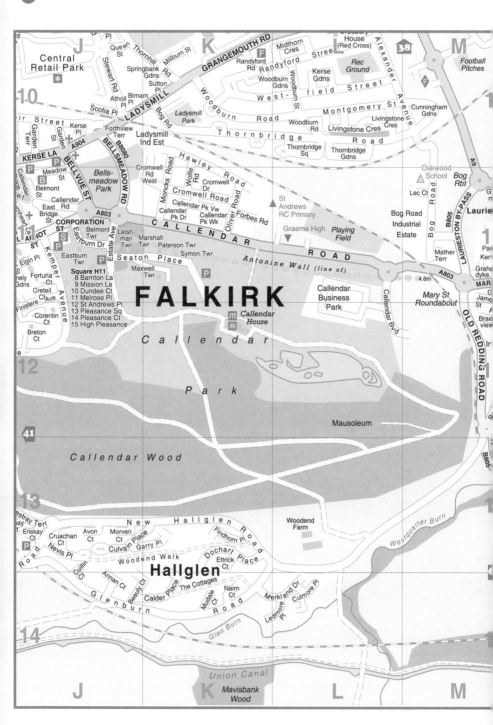

Central Retail Park

Football Pitches

GRANGEMOUTH RD

Queen St
Thornhill Rd
Millburn St
Pl
Randyford Rd
Randyford St
Midthorn Cres
Stree
Alexander Avenue
Bradbury House (Red Cross)
3S

Springbank Gdns
Sutton Pl
Birnam Pl
Atholl Pl
Scotia Pl
Stewart Rd
LADYSMILL
Woodburn Gdns
Woodburn St
West-
Kerse Gdns
field Street
Rec Ground

Bog Rd
Ladysmill Park
Ladysmill Ind Est
Woodburn Road
Montgomery St
Livingstone Cres
Woodburn Rd
Livingstone Cres
Cunningham Gdns

Kerse Garden Terr
ir Street
Kerse Pl
Garden St
Forthview Terr
A904
B8080
BELLSMEADOW RD
Thornbridge
Thornbridge Sq
Thornbridge Road
Thornbridge Gdns
A9

KERSE LA
Calendar Rise
Meadow St
Belmont St
Callendar East Rd
Bridge St
B
Bells-meadow Park
Cromwell Rd West
Moncks Road
Hawley Road
Wolfe Rd
Cromwell Dr
Cromwell Road
Oliver Road
Forbes Rd
St Andrews RC Primary
Oakwood School
Lec Ct
Bog Road
Bog Rbt
A9

CORPORATION ST
A803
Callendar Pk Dr
Callendar Pk Vw
Callendar Pk Wk
Graeme High
Playing Field
Bog Road Industrial Estate
B805
Laurie

L A NOT ST
S
P
Eastburn Dr
Estate Ave
Leishman Twr
Belmont Twr
Marshall Twr
Paterson Twr
Symon Twr
CALLENDAR
ROAD
Mather Terr
A803
MAR

Elgin Pl
Kemper Avenue
Eastburn Twr
Seaton Place
Maxwell Twr
Antonine Wall (line of)
Callendar Byd
4.6m
Mary St Roundabout
Grahamsdyke
Jame St
Brae view
Pa
Ker

nely Gdns
Fortuna Ct
Creteil Ct
Finistere Ct
ave
Corentin Ct
Breton Ct

Square H11
8 Barnton La
9 Mission La
10 Dundee Ct
11 Melrose Pl
12 St Andrews Pl
13 Pleasance Sq
14 Pleasance Ct
15 High Pleasance

P

FALKIRK

Callendar House

Callendar Business Park

Callendar

Park

41

Callendar Wood

Mausoleum

B805

13

estray Terr
Eriskay Ct
Road
Cruachan Ct
Nevis Pl
Avon Ct
Morven Ct
Culvain Place
Garry Pl
New Hallglen Road
Findhorn Pl
Dochart Place
Ettrick Ct
Woodend Walk
Cuillin Ct
Annan Ct
Beauly Ct
Hallglen
Calder Place
The Cottages
Mudale Ct
Nairn Ct
Merkland Dr
Ledmore Pl
Culmore Pl
Woodend Farm
Westquarter Burn

Glenburn
Road
Glen Burn

14

Union Canal
Mavisbank Wood

J K L M

sie Road	G12	Friendship Gardens	J4	Halket Crescent	J5	Kildrummy Avenue	F3
er Place	C3	Frobisher Avenue	F10	Hallam Road	D5	Kilmory Court	C11
lanrig Place	F2	Fulmar Crescent	C2	Hallglen Road	H14	Kilns Place	F9
rmond Place	F13	Gairdoch Drive	J4	Hallglen Terrace	H14	Kilns Road	G10
yat Place	F12	Gairdoch Street	H7	Hamilton Avenue	E3	Kincardine Road	J4
yat Rise	C2	Galbraith Crescent	C3	Hamilton Drive	G11	King Street	D5, F4
ar Avenue	F3	Galloway Court	H9	Hamilton Road	D2	(Stenhousemuir)	
an Avenue	H4	Galloway Street	H9	Hamilton Street	D9	King Street (Falkirk)	J9
arroch Street	B6	Garbett Place	G7	Harley Court	H7	Kings Court	D5
ee Court (10)	H11	Garden Street	J10	Harrison Place	E9	(Stenhousemuir)	
kirk)		Garden Terrace	J10	Haugh Gardens	H6	Kings Court (Laurieston)	H11
ee Court	G7	Garrison Place	H10	Haugh Street	H6	Kingseat Place	F12
ngal)		Garry Place	K13	Hawley Road	K10	Kingsley Avenue	F4
ee Place	G7	Gartcows Avenue	G11	Hawthorn Drive	E11	Kinnaird Avenue	H4
eld Place	J6	Gartcows Crescent	F12	Hawthorne Place	D6	Kinnaird Drive	E4
ing Place	J6	Gartcows Drive	G11	Hayfield Road	J8	Kintyre Place	C11
ottar Drive	F3	Gartcows Gardens	F11	Hayfield	J7	Kirk Avenue	E4
obin Avenue	F2	Gartcows Place	G12	Hazel Grove	K8	Kirk Wynd	H10
egan Avenue	F3	Gartcows Road	F12	Hedges, The	E10	Kirkton Cottages	K3
egan Drive	J6	Garthill Gardens	G11	Hendry Street	H8	Kirkton Place	J4
ey Place	B5	Garthill Lane	G11	Henryson Crescent	B5	Lade Drive	C7
Bridge Street	J11	Gascoigne Court	G7	Heritage Drive	G4	Ladeside Crescent	E6
Drive	C6	George Laing Court	E5	Heugh Street	G12	Ladysgate Court	H4
urn Drive	J11	George Street (Falkirk)	H10	High Pleasance (15)	H11	Ladysmill	J10
urn Tower	J11	George Street (Larbert)	C4	High Station Court	G12	Ladywell Court	A4
croft Street	B6	George Street	M11	High Station Road	G12	Lamond View	D6
rd Avenue	E3	(Laurieston)		High Street	H10	Langlees Street	J6
Place	J11	Gerald Terrace	E4	Highland Drive	C4	Larch Grove	F4
beth Avenue	C5	Gibsongray Street	G8	Hill o'Kinnaird Cottages	E1	Laurel Court	C9
beth Crescent	B9	Gilchrist Drive	E11	Hillary Road	D6	Laurieston By-Pass	M11
Place	B4	Gilfillan Place	J5	Hillcrest Road	F13	Lavery Avenue	B5
Terrace	G7	Gilsay Court	J13	Hillhead Drive	F13	Lawrence Court	B3
Grove	D6	Gladstone Road	D4	Hillview Road	C4	Learmonth Street	G11
ck Court	C2	Glasgow Road	B9	Hodge Street	H11	Lec Court	M11
ay Court	J13	Glebe Street	H10	Holly Avenue	F4	Ledmore Place	L14
he Lane	B5	Glen Brae	H12	Holyrood Place	E3	Leishman Tower	J11
e Avenue	J11	Glen Crescent	H14	Hope Street	H10	Lendrick Avenue	F13
Court	J8, K8	Glen Gardens	G12	Hornel Place	B5	Leny Crescent	G14
Road	J8	Glenbank	H14	Howard Street	F11	Leven Street	H7
k Court	K13	Glenbervie	A3	Howie's Place	B11	Lewis Court	H13
s Street	C4	Glenbervie Avenue	A4	Hunter Place	G3	Lime Grove	D6
Avenue	H8	Glenbervie Drive	A4	Hurworth Street	F12	Lime Road	B11
g Drive	H8	Glenbrae Court	H12	Inch Colm Avenue	C3	Linlithgow Place	E3
Place	H8	Glenburn Road	J14	Inch Garvie Terrace	C2	Lint Riggs	H10
eld Place	J9	Glencairn Street	B10	Inchkeith Place	H13	Lionthorn Court	F13
y Place	A4	Glenfuir Court	D11	Inglis Drive	J5	Lionthorn Road	E14
e Drive	C10	Glenfuir Road	D11	Innerpeffray Drive	G4	Lismore Court	H13
e Gardens	D10	Glenfuir Street	C10	Inver Court	J6	Livingstone Crescent	L10
e Street	C10	Glengarry Crescent	F13	Inverary Drive	F2	Loch View	A6
n Drive	B4	Glenochil Road	G12	Iona Place	H13	Lochaber Drive	F4
k Road	B6, B7	Glentye Gardens	E12	Irving Court	E10	Lochgreen Road	E13
bert)		Glenview Drive	F13	Islands Crescent	H13	Lochlands Avenue	B7
k Road	H13	Glynwed Court	J8	Jacob Place	H12	Lochlands Loan	A8
n Village)		Godfrey Crescent	C6	James Croft Drive	F14	Lochmaben Drive	F3
k Road	M9	Gordon Place	E10	James Short Park	H12	Lodge Drive	F5
rieston)		Goshen Place	E5	James Street (Larbert)	D5	Logie Drive	A4
and Place	E3	Gowan Avenue	H9	James Street (Falkirk)	H9	Lomond Crescent	E4
Street	G6	Gowan Lane	H9	James Street	M11	Lomond Drive	J6
tharson Way	F14	Gradlon Place	H12	(Laurieston)		Longdales Avenue	G7
uson Drive	G2	Graeme Place	E13	Jamieson Avenue	E4	Longdales Court	G7
Lea Grove	J4	Graham Avenue	B4	Jarvie Place	G6	Longdales Place	G7
orn Place	K13	Grahams Road	H9	John o'Hara Court	D10	Longdales Road	G7
ere Avenue	H12	Grahamsdyke Street	M11	John Street	H8	Longdyke Place	J3
rig Court	F3	Granary Road	G7	Johnston Avenue	F4	Lorimar Place	H5
yson Place	C2	Granary Square	H8	Johnston Court	G7	Lorne Road	C5
ane	D6	Grange Avenue	K9	Jones Avenue	C7	MacAdam Place	D9
Street	J9	Grange Drive	K9	Keir Hardie Avenue	M12	McCambridge Place	C2
ng Drive	G4	Grange View	E5	Kemper Avenue	H12	McCartney Road	C3
ng Gardens	E9	Grangemouth Road	K10	Kenilworth Drive	M11	McCormack Place	D3
es Court	L9	Greenbank Court	D11	Kenmuir Street	A10	MacDonald Court	B2
s Crescent	D6	Greenbank Place	D11	Kenmure Place	F3	McDonald Crescent	J8
es Road	K11	Greenbank Road	D11	Kennard Street	J9	MacFarlane Crescent	H10
vce Gardens	E11	Greenhorn's Well Avenue	F12	Keppock Place	F13	McGhee Place	F13
Avenue	B4	Greenhorn's Well	F11	Kerse Gardens	L10	McGowan Road	J8
view Court	F13	Crescent		Kerse Lane	J10	McInally Crescent	F7
view Terrace	J10	Greenhorn's Well Drive	F12	Kerse Place	J10	MacIntosh Place	G14
na Court	J11	Grenville Court	F10	Kersehill Circle	J8	McIntyre Avenue	C2
dry Loan	B5	Griffiths Court	H11	Kersehill Crescent	J8	McKell Court	G12
dry Street	G7	Grove Crescent	G5	Kilbean Drive	F13	MacKenzie Place	G13
shi Drive	F2	Guthrie Crescent	B5	Kilbrennan Drive	B11	McLachlan Street	C5

Index to street names is continued on page 46

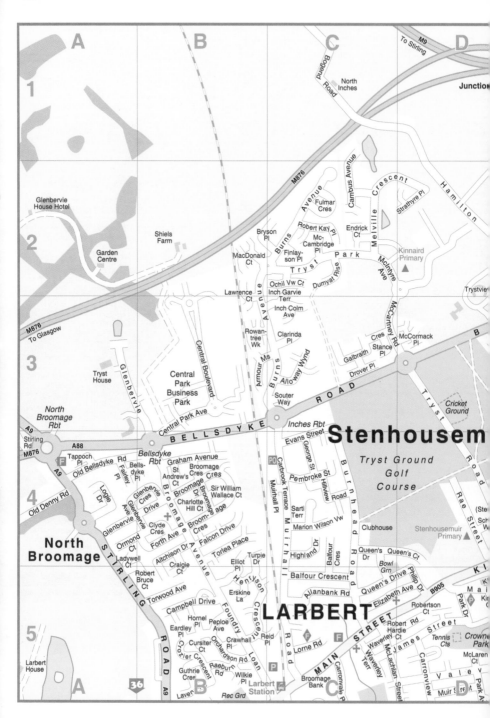

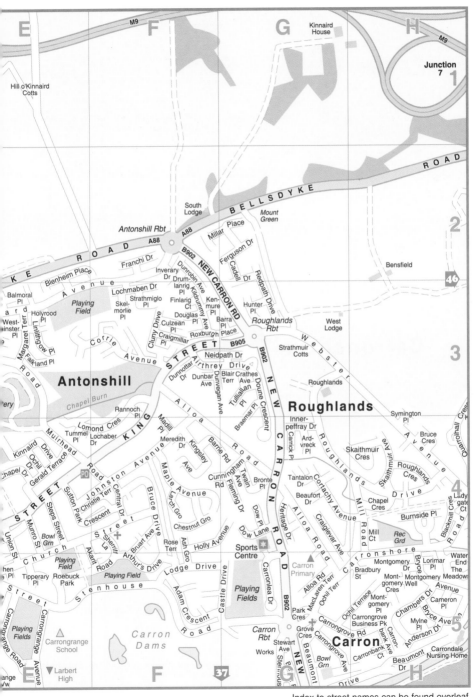

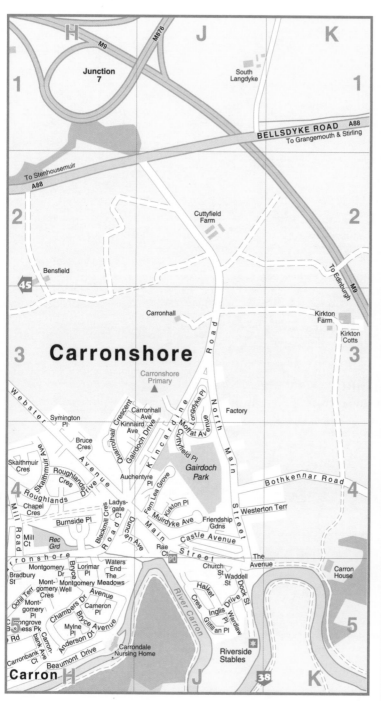

rhead Road	E3	Quarrolhall Crescent	H4	South Pleasance	H11	Universal Road	L8
och Avenue	G7	Queen Street	J10	Avenue		Upper Newmarket	H10
ngal Mill Court	F7	Queen's Court	D4	South View	D6	Street	
ngal Place	G7	Queen's Crescent	F10	Spinkhill	M13	Valeview	D5
ngalend Court	H8	Queen's Drive (Falkirk)	F10	Springbank Gardens	K10	Valley View Drive	G7
ngalend	H8	Queen's Drive (Larbert)	C4	Springfield Drive	F10	Valley View Place	G8
ngalhead Road	G8	Rae Court	J4	Staffa Place	H13	Vanachar Road	G14
nro Street	E4	Rae Street	D4	Stance Place	C3	Vicar Street	H10
ray Court	G11	Raeburn Road	B5	Stark Avenue	D10	Victoria Road (Larbert)	B6
ne Place	H5	Raleigh Court	E10	Stenhouse Road	F5	Victoria Road (Falkirk)	J9
eton Way	F12	Ramsay Avenue	M12	Stephen's Croft	F7	Waddell Street	J5
er Road	E9	Randyford Road	K10	Steps Street	E4	Waggon Road	H8
n Court	K14	Randyford Street	L10	Stevenson Court	H6	Wall Gardens	C9
ier Crescent	G8	Rannoch Place	F3	Stewart Avenue	G5	Wall Street	C9
ier Place	G8	Redbrae Road	D9	Stewart Road	J10	Wallace Buildings	H9
lpath Drive	F3	Redding Road	M12	Stirling Road	A4, D8	Wallace Place	J9
son Street	H11	Redpath Drive	G3	Strachan Street	D11	Wallace Street	H9
is Place	J13	Reid Place	B5	Strathmiglo Place	F3	Wardlaw Place	J5
Carron Road	F2, G6	Rennie Street	G11	Strathmuir Cottages	G3	Waterfurs Drive	G7
Hallglen Road	H13	River Street	G6	Strathyre Place	D2	Waters End	H5
carron Court	G7	Robert Bruce Court	B5	(Stenhousemuir)		Watling Avenue	C10
house Drive	E13	Robert Hardie Court	D5	Strathyre Place	G14	Watling Drive	D10
market Street	H10	Robert Kay Place	C2	(Falkirk)		Watling Gardens	D9
olson Place	F13	Robertson Court	D5	Striven Drive	J6	Watling Street	C9
h Main Street	J4	Roebuck Park	E5	Styles Place	F13	Watson Street	H10
h Street	H7	Roman Drive	D10	Summerford	D11	Watt Gardens	E9
hern Distributor	J7	Ronades Road	G8	Summerford Gardens	D11	Waverley Road	C5
ad		Ronald Crescent	B6	Summerford Road	D11	Waverley Street	H7
sery Road	E11	Rose Terrace	F4	Sunnylaw Place	F12	Waverley Terrace	C5
Drive	D6	Rosebank Avenue	F10	Sunnyside Road	F10	Webster Avenue	G3
l Drive	E4	Rosebank Place	F10	Sunnyside Street	E9	Wee Row	H9
l Terrace	G5	Rosehall Terrace	H11	Sutton Park Crescent	E4	Weir Street	J10
View Court	C2	Ross Crescent	C10	Sutton Place	K10	Well Road	F12
ltree Terrace	A10	Roughlands Crescent	H4	Sword's Way	G6	Wellside Court	G10
ltree Terrace	B10	Roughlands Drive	G4	Symington Place	H3	Wellside Place	G10
lview Court	E4	Roundel, The	K8	Symon Tower	K11	Wellside Terrace	H10
Bellsdyke Road	A4	Rowan Crescent	A11	Tait Drive	C7	West Bridge Street	G10
Denny Road	A4	Rowantree Walk	B3	Tamfourhill Avenue	C11	West Drive	C6
Redding Road	M11	Roxburgh Place	F3	Tamfourhill Road	C11	West Mains Road	M8
er Road	K11	Russel Street	H10	Tanera Court	H13	Westburn Avenue	E11
ard Street	J10	Russell Hill Court	B6	Tanners Road	G10	Westerglen Road	G13
ardhall Avenue	J7	St Andrew's Court	B4	Tantalon Drive	G4	Western Avenue	H9
ardhall Drive	J7	St Andrews Place (12)	H11	Tappoch Place	A4	Westerton Terrace	J4
ardhall Way	J7	St Crispin's Place	H11	Tay Street	J6	Westfield Street	L10
ardson Road	B5	St David's Court	B6	Taylor Court	J8	Westminster Place	E3
ey Place	H13	St George's Court	B6	Taylor's Road	C6	Westpark Court	F7
ond Court	A4	St Giles Square	B9	Telford Square	E9	Westpark Crescent	F7
orne Gardens	F12	St Giles Way	B9	Teviot Street	F11	Westray Terrace	J13
orne Street	F12	St John's Avenue	J9	Thistle Street	J9	Whitegates Place	C11
ald Street	H11	St John's Court	J9	Thomson Crescent	E12	Wilkie Place	B5
ovan Place	F9	St Modans Court	H11	Thornbridge Gardens	L10	Williamson Avenue	G6
Avenue (Larbert)	D5	Sainford Crescent	G6	Thornbridge Road	K10	Williamson Place	J8
Avenue (Laurieston)	M11	Salmon Drive	E13	Thornbridge Square	L10	Williamson Street	H11
Crescent	G5	Sarti Terrace	C4	Thorndene Court	F13	Wilson Avenue	C10
Drive	D5	School Walk	D4	Thornhill Court	J9	Wilson Drive	C10
Road	G6	Scotia Place	J10	Thornhill Road	J9	Wilson Gardens	C9
Street	H10	Scott Terrace	H6	Tipperary Place	E5	Wilson Road	C9
View Court	E10	Seafield Court	F13	Tiree Place	H13	Wilsons Close (7)	H11
foot Court	H12	Seaforth Road	J6	Tolbooth Street (4)	H11	Windsor Avenue	E11
head Cottages	H13	Seaton Place	J11	Tophill Entry	F9	Windsor Crescent	E11
head Road	H14	Shannon Drive	F11	Torlea Place	B4	Windsor Drive	F11
view Avenue	F13	Sherriff Lane	F4	Torridon Avenue	J6	Windsor Gardens	F11
rson Tower	K11	Shiel Gardens	J6	Torwood Avenue	B5	Windsor Road	D11, E11
oroke Street	C4	Simpson Street	E9	Towers Court	H9	Wolfe Road	K11
lers Lane	G10	Sinclair Place	G6	Tryst Park	C2	Woodburn Street	L10
Drive	D5	Sir John Graham Court	B6	Tryst Road	D3	Woodburn Gardens	L10
Street	H8	Sir William Wallace	B4	Trystpark	D3	Woodburn Road	K10
Walk	D6	Court		Trystview	D2	Woodend Walk	H13, J13
rhill Gardens	G13	Skaithmuir Avenue	H4	Tulliallan Place	G3	Woodlands	G11
sance	H11	Skaithmuir Crescent	H4	Tummel Place	E4	Crescent	
sance Court (14)	H11	Skelmorlie Place	F3	Turpie Drive	B4	Woodside Court	H12
sance Gardens	H11	Skython Way	E13	Twain Avenue	G4	Woodside Grove	D7
sance Road	H11	Slamannan Road	E13	Union Gardens	E10	Woodside Terrace	H11
sance Square (13)	H11	Smith Street	H8	Union Place	B6	Wooer Street (5)	H11
ownie	D10	Souter Way	C3	Union Road	D10	Wright Street	H9
ria Road	B6	South Bantaskine Drive	G12	Union Street	E4	Yardley Place	G6
es Street	H10	South Bantaskine Road	G12	(Stenhousemuir)		York Drive	K9
ect Street	E10	South Broomage Avenue	C6	Union Street	H8	York Street	K9
ecthill Road	G13	South Melville Lane (3)	H10	(Falkirk)			

Index to Fallin

Alexander McLeod Place	D4	Cory's Court	D3	Hirst Court	C3	Sinclair Drive	
Balure Crescent	C3	Dr Porter Gardens	C3	Hirst Crescent	C3	Square, The	
Bandeath Road	C3	Farm Road	C3	King Street	B3	Steadings, The	
Bannock Road	A3	Forth Street	B3	Lamont Crescent	C3	Stirling Road	A2,
Baxter Street	C3	Gracie Crescent	C3	Moss Road	B3	Wallace Place	
Beda Place	B2	Hardie Crescent	B3	Oak Drive	C3	Weir Drive	
Bruce Drive	B2	Hawthorn Crescent	C3	Ochil Street	B3	Woodside Place	
Castle View	C3	Hawthorn Drive	B3	Polmaise Crescent	B2		
Colliers Road	C3	Hilton Terrace	B3	Polmaise Park	C3		
		Hillview Place	A3	Queen Street	B3		

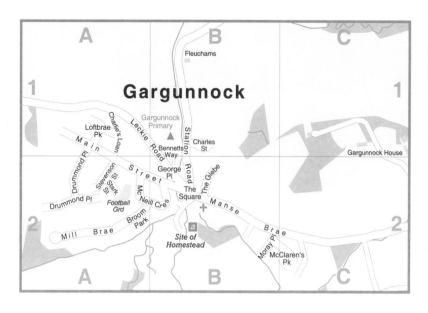

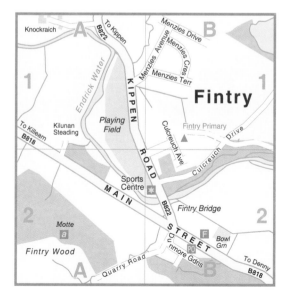

Index to Gargunnock

Bennetts Way	B1
Broom Park	A2
Charles Street	B1
Charlie's Loan	A1
Drummond Place	A2
George Place	B2
Glebe, The	B2
Leckie Road	A1
Loftbrae Park	A1
McClaren's Park	C2
McNeill Crescent	A2
Main Street	A1
Manse Brae	B2
Mill Brae	A2
Moray Place	B2
Square, The	B2
Stark Street	A2
Station Road	B1
Stevenson Street	A2

Index to Fintry

Culcreuch Avenue	B1
Culcreuch Drive	B2
Dunmore Gardens	B2
Kilunan Steading	A1
Kippen Road	A1
Main Street	A2
Menzies Avenue	B1
Menzies Crescent	B1
Menzies Drive	B1
Menzies Terrace	B1
Quarry Road	A2

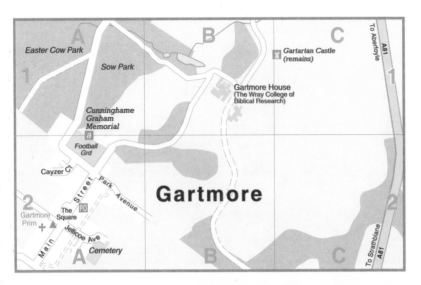

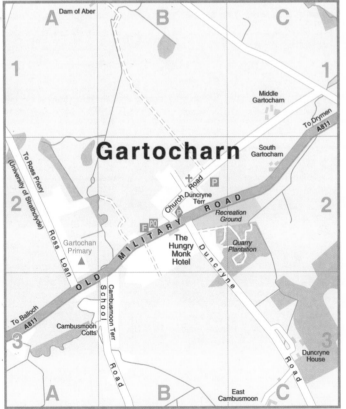

Index to Gartmore

Index to Gartocharn

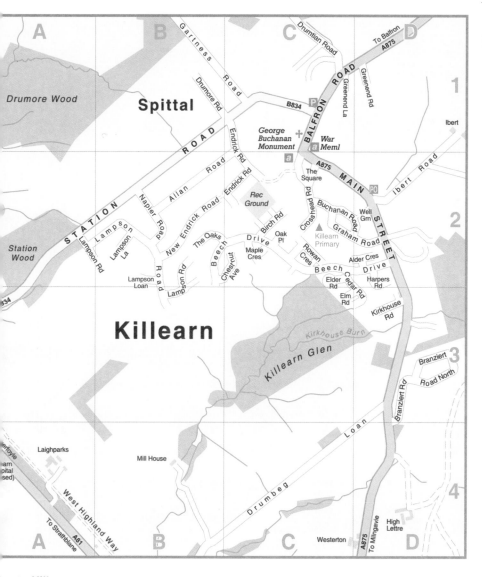

ex to Killearn

r Crescent	D2	Crosshead Road	C2	Greenend Road	D1	New Endrick Road	B2
Road	B2	Drumbeg Loan	C4	Harpers Road	D2	Oak Place	C2
on Road	C1	Drumore Road	B1	Ibert Road	D2	Oaks, The	B2
h Drive	C2	Drumtian Road	C1	Kirkhouse Road	D3	Rowan Crescent	C2
Road	C2	Elder Road	C2	Lampson Lane	B2	Square, The	C2
ziert Road North	D3	Elm Road	C3	Lampson Loan	B2	Station Road	A2
ziert Road	D3	Endrick Road	C1	Lampson Road	A2, B2	Well Green	D2
anan Road	C2	Gartness Road	B2	Main Street	D2		
r Road	C2	Graham Road	C2	Maple Crescent	C2		
stnut Avenue	C2	Greenend Lane	C1	Napier Road	B2		

B   C   D   E

Howkerse

Brackenlees   Road

Thistlebank

Pinfoldbridge

Newton Road

1

Bothkennar
Rd

Teindsyard

CORONATION PL.

Bothkennar
Primary

Potter
Pl

Skinflats

Zetland Pl

2

Campie Terr

Newton   Avenue

Edward
Pl

Rec
Grd

Binnie
Pl

Newton Road

3

Yonderhaugh

River Carron

To Stirling

Kerse
Bridge

Kerse
Bridge

Middle St La

Wareho

M9

North
Bridge
St

Glensburgh

South Bridge

Gr

4

Lock

Pipe Bridge

GLENSBURGH ROAD

Devon Street

Avon Street

Don Street

Tweed Street

Bank St

Kelvin Street

Clyde St

West
Church
Dr

Kerse
Vw

Road

Way

McCafferty
Way

Ti

Marina

Dalgrain
Park

Tay St

Dalgrain

Forth-Clyde

EARL'S   ROAD

A9

36

Playing
Field

Zetland
Dr

Rugby
Ground

Lock

5

Recreation
Ground

Chemical
Works

Earl's Road
Industrial
Estate

Forth & Clyde Canal

Hotel

A905

EARL'S

A904

E

B

56

To Edinburgh

M9

C

Bowl
Grn

D

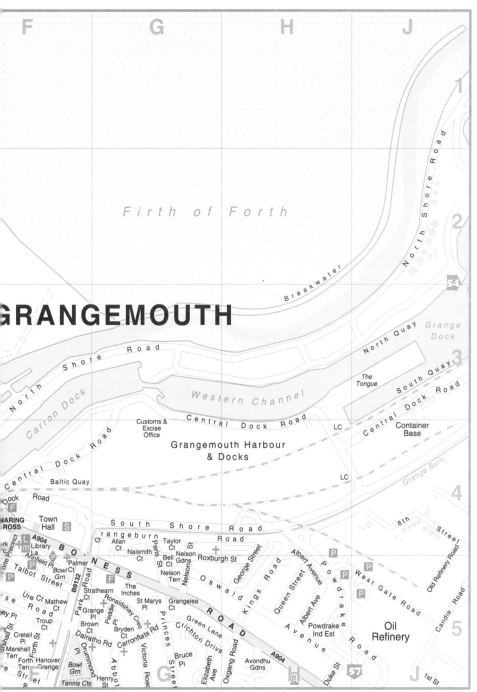

F **G** **H** **J**

1

Firth of Forth

North Shore Road

2

54

Breakwater

North Quay *Grange Dock*

GRANGEMOUTH

North Shore Road

The Tongue

South Quay 3

North

Carron Dock

Western Channel

Central Dock Road

Central Dock Road

Container Base

Customs & Excise Office

Grangemouth Harbour & Docks

LC

Central Dock Road

Grange Burn

Baltic Quay

LC 4

Dock Road

F

HARING CROSS

Town Hall S

South Shore Road

Road

6th Street

Old Refinery Road

L A904
Library
La

Grangeburn

Allan Ct

Taylor Ct

Nelson Gdns

Roxburgh St

George Street

Albert Avenue

P

West Gate Road

P

Candie Road

Annfield Pl

Palmer

Bowl Ct
Grn

Naismith Ct

Paris St

Bell Ct

Nelson St

Kings Road

Queen Street

Powdrake Road

P

P

Talbot Street

B9132

Strathearn Ct

The Inches

Nelson Terr

Oswald

Oxgang Road

Oil Refinery

Ure Ct

Mathew Ct

Ronaldshay Cres

St Marys Pl

Grangelea Ct

Albert Ave

Powdrake Ind Est

Grange Pl

Peddie St

Princes Street

Green Lane

Road

Avenue

Troup Ct

Brown Ct

Bryden Ct

Crichton Drive

A904

Creteil Pl

Dalratho Rd

Carronflats Rd

Victoria Road

Elizabeth Ave

Avondhu Gdns

Duke St

57

1st St

Marshall Terr

Forth Hanover Ter Grange

Drummond Pl

Bruce Pl

J

Bowl Grn

Henry St

Tennis Cts

F G

Index to street names can be found overleaf

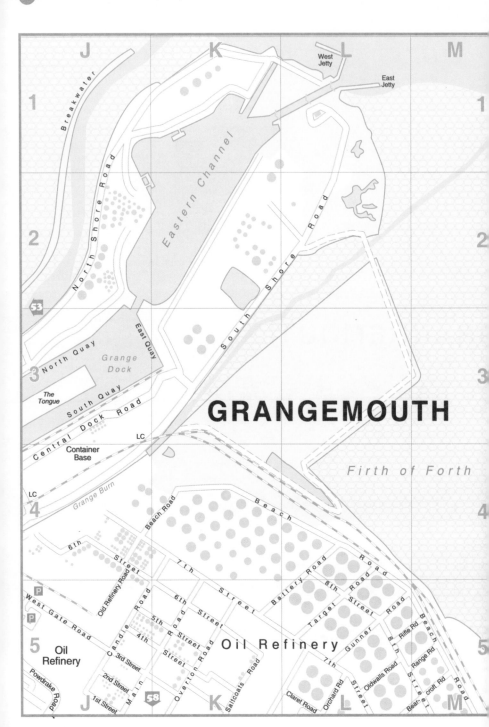

J   K   L   M

1

West Jetty

East Jetty

Breakwater

North Shore Road

Eastern Channel

2

South Shore Road

53

North Quay

East Quay

Grange Dock

3

The Tongue

South Quay

Central Dock Road

Container Base

LC

GRANGEMOUTH

Firth of Forth

LC

Grange Burn

4

Beach Road

Beach Road

6th

Street

Old Refinery Road

7th Street

Battery Road

8th Street

Road

Target Road

Street

Gunner

Road

P

P

West Gate Road

Candie Road

5th Road Street

6th Road Street

Oil Refinery

7th Street

Rifle Rd

8th Street

Beach

Range Rd

5

Oil Refinery

4th Street

3rd Street

Main

Street

Overton Road

Saltcoats Road

Orchard Rd

Oldwalls Road

Bear-croft Rd

Road

Powdrake Road

2nd Street

58

1st Street

Claret Road

J   K   L   M

...ex to Grangemouth & Skinflats

...reet	J6	Bowhouse Road	F8, G7	Devon Street	C4	Inches, The	F5
				Dochart Path	F4	Inchyra Place	H7
...treet (Oil Ref)	J5	Bowhouse Square	F8	Dock Road	F4	Inchyra Road	H7, H8
...treet (Chem Wks)	M7	Boyd Street	C10	Don Street	C4	Islay Court	F8
...treet (Oil Ref)	J5	Brackenlees Road	B1	Douglas Avenue	G7	Jackson Avenue	F6
...treet (Chem Wks)	M7	Brae Road	M7	Drummond Park	F7	James Street	B10
...treet (Oil Ref)	J5	Braeside Place	D9	Drummond Place	F5	James Cornwall	H6
...reet (Chem Wks)	N7	Braeview	B10	Dryburgh Way	H7	Court	
...treet (Oil Ref)	K5	Bravo Street	N8	Duke Street	H5	Jasper Avenue	C10
...reet	N7	Briardene	C10	Dundas Crescent	C10	Jinkabout Road	M9
...em Wks)		Brooke Lane	E8	Dundas Road	C10	Jura Place	F8
...treet (Oil Ref)	J4, K5	Brooke Street	E8	Dundas Street	E5	Kelvin Street	C4
...reet	N7	Brown Court	F5	Earl's Road	D5	Kenilworth Drive	B9
...m Wks)		Bruce Place	G5	Earn Court	F8	Kenilworth Lane	E8
...treet (Oil Ref)	K4, L5	Bruce Road	N8	East Road	L8	Kenilworth Street	E8
...reet	N8	Bryden Court	G5	Eddystone Court	H7	Kerse Road	F5
...em Wks)		Buchan Place	E8	Edward Place	B2	Kerse View	D4
...reet	L5	Buchan Road	M7	Elizabeth Avenue	G6	Kersiebank Avenue	G7
...sford Drive	H7	Burnbank Road	F7, F8	Elmbank Street	E7	King's Road	H5
...angemouth)		Burnfoot Court	F7	Erbach Avenue	D9	Kingseat Avenue	F7
...sford Drive	C9	Burns Avenue	F8	Ettrick Court	G7	Kinloch Place	G8
...rieston)		Burns Crescent	B9	Falkirk Road	B7	La Porte Precinct	F5
...sgrange Road	G5, G6	Bute Place	F7	Fendoch Road	H6	Larch Street	E7
...sinch Court	H6	Cairngorm Road	G8	Fintry Road	G9	Laurieston By-pass	C9
...sinch Road	H6	Caledon Green	D6	Flare Road	K8	Laurieston Road	C7
...s Road	F6	Callendar Boulevard	A10	Forth Street	F5	Laurmont Court (2)	C10
...airney Place	G6	Callendar Road	A9	Forth Terrace	F5	Lawers Place	G8
...t Avenue	H5	Campie Terrace	B2	Forth-Clyde Way	C5	Lec Court	B9
...nder Avenue	E8	Campsie Road	G8	Forties Road	M8	Lennox Terrace	H8
...vhouse)		Candie Crescent	G7	Fraser Place	F7	Library Lane	F4
...nder Avenue	A8	Candie Road	J5	Fullarton Drive	G10	Lime Street	E6
...dlefield)		Carbrook Place	G7	Garry Place	G8	Livingstone Crescent	A8
...Court	G4	Carron Place	F8	George Street	H5	Loanhead Avenue	G7
...nd Court	E7	Carronflats Road	G5	(Grangemouth)		Lomond Road	G8
...nd Pow	F6	Carse Crescent	C9	George Street	B10	Lorne Gardens	B10
...nd Street	E7	Castleton Crescent	F7	(Laurieston)		Lumley Court	F5
...Street	N8	Cedar Street	F6	Glenbervie Road	H7	Lumley Place	F5
...rley Path	H7	Central Avenue	E7	Glensburgh Road	C4	Lumley Street	F5
...eld Place	F5	Central Dock Road	F4, J3	Glenside Court	G7	MacKenzie Court	E7
...ourt	F8	Charing Cross	F4	Gort Place	E8	MacKenzie Terrace	E7
...Court	F7	Charlotte Dundas	G7	Grahamsdyke Street	B9, C9	McCafferty Way	E4
...Crescent	D10	Court		Grampian Crescent	G8	Magnus Road	M8
...Drive	B10	Cheviot Place	G8	Grange Lane	E4	Main Road	J5
...bank Avenue	G7	Chisholm Place	D7	Grange Place	F5	Marmion Road	F8
...Road	M6	Claret Road (Bowhouse)	G7	Grange Road	H9	Marshall Street	F5
...Street	C4	Claret Road (Oil Ref)	L5	Grangeburn Road	G4	Marshall Terrace	F5
...dale Road	K10	Clyde Street	D4	Grangelea Court	F5	Mary Square	C10
...dhu Gardens	H5	Coll Place	F7	Grangemouth Road	M8	Mary Street	B9
...oral Road	N7	Compton Road	E8	Green Lane	G5	Maryflats Place	G6
...Street	C4	Compressor House	K8	Gunn Road	E8	Mather Terrace	B9
...hill Court	F7	Road		Gunner Road	L5	Mathew Court	F5
...e Place	F8	Coronation Place	B2	Haig Street	E7	Melrose Drive	H7
...ry Road	L5	Cotton Lane	C10	Haining Place	H6	Merrick Road	H8
...h Road	J4, M5	Craigleith Road	F7	Hamilton Road	G7	Merrick Way	G8
...cross Road	D6, E8	Creteil Place	F5	Hanover Grange	F5	Miller Road	N8
...croft Gardens	G6	Crichton Drive	G5	Harris Place	E8	Millhall Gardens	H10
...croft Road	L6	Croftside Court	G7	Hartley Place	D7	Middle Street Lane	E4
...y Court	F8	Cruachan Place	H8	Hawthorn Street	E7	Montgomery Street	E7
...h Place	E7	Cruden Road	M8	Hayworth Avenue	D9	(Bowhouse)	
...Court	G5	Cuillin Place	G8	Hazel Road	E7	Montgomery Street	A8
...hill Crescent	G7	Cultenhove Crescent	G7	Henry Street	G5	(Middlefield)	
...e Place	B3	Cunningham Gardens	B8	Hornbeam Crescent	C10	Morar Court	F8
...Road	B9	Cunningham Street	E8	Icehouse Brae	C8	Morar Place	F8
...ss Road	F4, H10	Dalgrain Road	C4	(North)		Moray Place	G6
...ennar Road	B1	Dalratho Road	F5	Icehouse Brae	D9	Moriston Court	G9
				(South)		Mossgiel Terrace	C10

Index to street names continued on page 59.

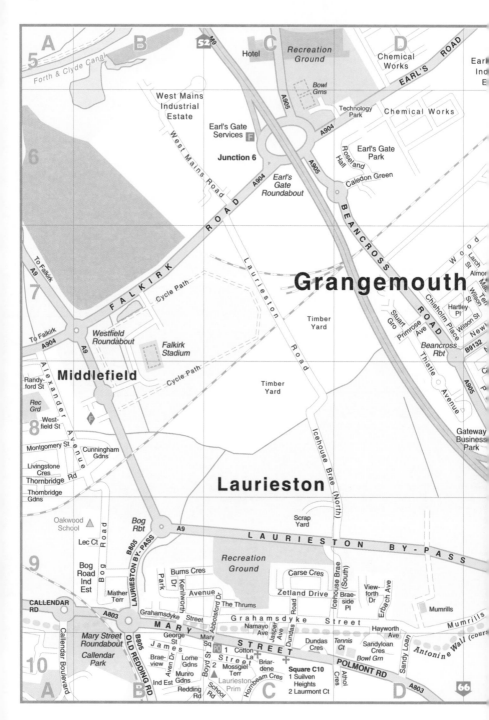

A B 52 C Hotel Recreation Ground Chemical Works D Earl's Ind E

5

Forth & Clyde Canal

West Mains Industrial Estate

West Mains Road

Earl's Gate Services F

Junction 6

6

Earl's Gate Roundabout

Earl's Gate Park

Technology Park

Chemical Works

Roseland Hall

Caledon Green

FALKIRK ROAD

Laurieston Road

Cycle Path

Grangemouth

To Falkirk A9

7

Timber Yard

BEANCROSS ROAD

EARL'S ROAD

Wood Larch Almo Mal Ter Wilson

Chisholm Place

Hartley Pl Wilson St

Stuart Gro Primrose Ave Thistle Ave

Beancross Rbt

B9132

Newl

A905

To Falkirk A904

Westfield Roundabout

Falkirk Stadium

Cycle Path

Alexander Avenue

A9

Middlefield

Randy-ford St

Rec Grd

West-field St

Montgomery St

Livingstone Cres

Thornbridge Gdns

Cunningham Gdns

Rd

8

Timber Yard

Gateway Business Park

Laurieston

Icehouse Brae (North)

Oakwood School

Lec Ct

Bog Road

Bog Rbt

A9

LAURIESTON BY-PASS

Scrap Yard

Recreation Ground

Burns Cres

Carse Cres

Zetland Drive

Icehouse Brae (South)

Braeside Pl

Viewforth Dr

Erbach Ave

Mumrills

Mumril

9

Bog Road Ind Est

Mather Terr

LAURIESTON BY-PASS

B805

Park

Kenilworth Dr

Avenue

Abbotsford Dr

The Thrums

Grahamsdyke Street

CALLENDAR RD

A803

Mary Street Roundabout

Callendar Park

Callendar Boulevard

OLD REDDING RD B805

MARY STREET

George St

James

Grahamsdyke

Brae-view Dr

Aven Dr

Lorne Gdns

Munro Gdns

Ind Est

Redding Rd

School Rd

Mary Sq

Bog Rd

Mossgiel Terr

Laurieston Prim

PO

1 Cotton La

Briardene

Hornbeam Cres

Namayo Ave

Jasper Ave

Dundas Road

Square C10
1 Suilven Heights
2 Laurmont Ct

Dundas Cres

Tennis Ct

Hayworth Ave

Sandyloan Cres

Bowl Grn

Athol Cres

POLMONT RD

Antonine Wall (cours

Sandy Loan

10

A B C D A803 66

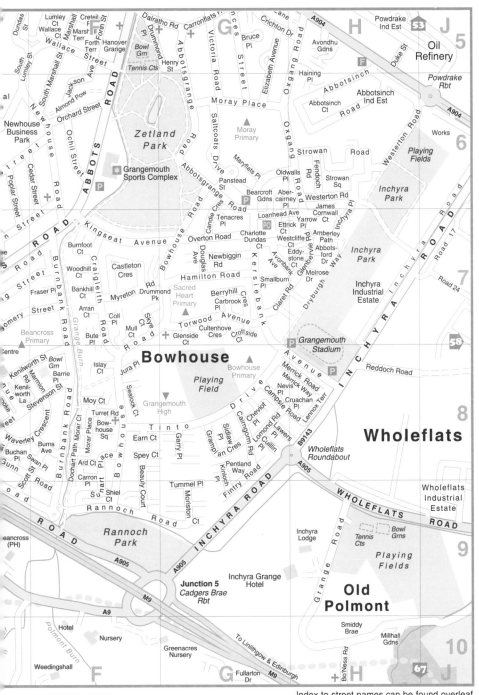

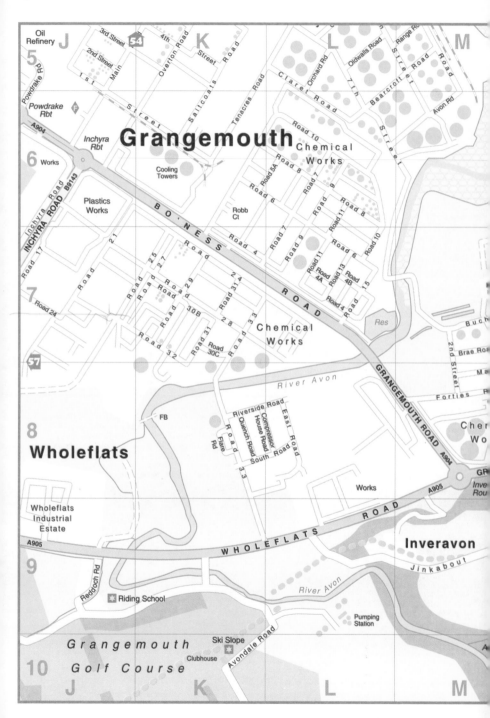

Index to Grangemouth & Skinflats cont...

Mountbatten Street	E8	Road 11	L7	Tummel Place	G9
Moy Court	F8	Road 13	L7	Turret Road	F8
Mull Court	F7	Road 15	L7	Tweed Street	C4
Mumrills Road	D9	Road 17	J7	Union Road	F5
Munro Gardens	B10	Road 21	J7	Ure Court	F5
Myreton Road	F7	Road 24	J7	Victoria Road	G5
Naismith Court	G4	Road 25	J7	Viewforth Drive	D9
Namayo Avenue	C9	Road 27	K7	Wallace Court	F5
Nelson Gardens	G4	Road 28	K7	Wallace Street	F5
Nelson Road	N7	Road 29	K7	Wavell Street	E8
Nelson Street	G5	Road 30B	K7	Waverley Crescent	E8
Nelson Terrace	G5	Road 30C	K7	West Church Drive	D4
Nevis Place	G8	Road 31	K7	West Gate Road	J5
Newbiggin Road	G7	Road 32	K7	West Mains Road	B6
Newhouse Road	F6	Road 33	K7, K8	Westcliffe Court	H7
Newlands Road	E7	Robb Court	K6	Westfield Street	A8
Newton Avenue	B2	Rodney Street	E7	Westerton Road	H6
Newton Road	C1, C3	Ronaldshay Crescent	G5	Wholeflats Road	H9
Ninian Road	N7	Roseland Hall	D6	Wilson Street	E7
North Bridge Street	E4	Roxburgh Street	G5	Wood Street	D7
North Shore Road	F3, J2	St Marys Place	G5	Woodhill Court	F7
Ochil Street	F6	Saltcoats Drive	G6	Yarrow Place	H7
Old Redding Road	B10	Saltcoats Road	K6	York Arcade	F4
Old Refinery Road	J5	Sandyloan Crescent	D10	York Lane	F4
Oldwalls Place	G6	Sandy Loan	D10	York Square	F4
Oldwalls Road	L5	School Road	C10	Zetland Drive	C5
Orchard Road	L5	Scott Street	E9	(Glensburgh)	
Orchard Street	F6	Sealock Court	F8	Zetland Drive	C9
Oswald Avenue	H5	Sharp Terrace	E7	(Laurieston)	
Overton Road	G7, K5	Shaw Place	E8	Zetland Place	B2
Oxgang Road	H6	Shiel Court	F9		
Palmer Court	F5	Sidlaw Place	G8		
Panstead Street	G6	Skye Court	F7		
Paris Street	G4	Smallburn Place	G7		
Park Avenue	B9	Smiddy Brae	H10		
Park Road	F5	South Bridge Street	E4		
Peddie Place	G5	South Lumley Street	E6		
Pentland Way	G8	South Marshall Street	F6		
Polmont Road	D10	South Road	K8		
Poplar Street	E6	South Shore Road	G7, K3		
Portal Road	E8	Spey Court	F8		
Potter Place	B2	Station Road	F4		
Powdrake Road	H5	Stevenston Street	F8		
Primrose Avenue	D7	Strathearn Court	F5		
Princes Street	G5	Strowan Road	H6		
Queen Street	H5	Strowan Square	H6		
Quench Road	K8	Stuart Grove	D7		
Randyford Street	A8	Suilven Heights (1)	C10		
Range Road	M5	Sunart Place	F9		
Rannoch Road	F9	Swan Place	F8		
Redding Road	B10	Talbot Street	F5		
Reddoch Road	H8, J9	Target Road	L5		
Rifle Road	L5	Tay Street	C4		
Ritchie Place	E8	Taylor Court	G4		
Riverside Road	K8	Tedder Street	E8		
Road 4	L7	Tenacres Place	G7		
Road 4A	L7	Tenacres Road	K6		
Road 4B	L7	Thistle Avenue	D7		
Road 5A	K6	Thornbridge Gardens	A8		
Road 6	K6, L7	Thornbridge Road	A8		
Road 7	L6, L7	Thrums, The	C9		
Road 8	L6	Tinto Drive	G8		
Road 9	L6, L7	Torwood Avenue	G7		
Road 10	L7	Troup Court	F5		

Sewage
Works

6th Street
Nelson Rd
7th Street
Road

Road

Bo'ness
A904

s & Kinneil
ilway

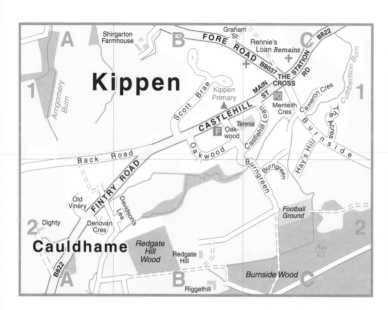

Index to Kippen

Acres, The
Back Road
Burngreen
Burnside
Cameron Crescent
Castlehill
Castlehill Loan
Cross, The
Davidson's Lea
Denovan Crescent
Fintry Road
Fore Road
Graham Street
Hay's Hill
Main Street
Menteith Crescent
Oakwood
Old Vinery
Rennie's Loan
Scott Brae
Station Road

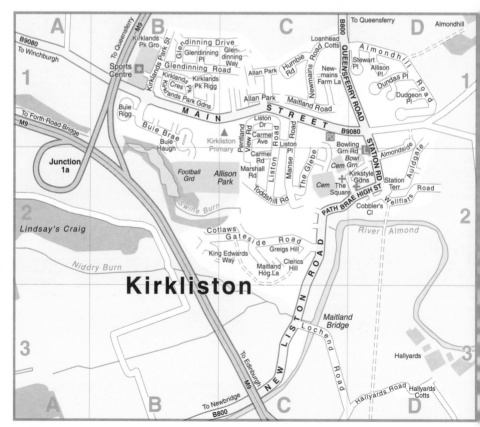

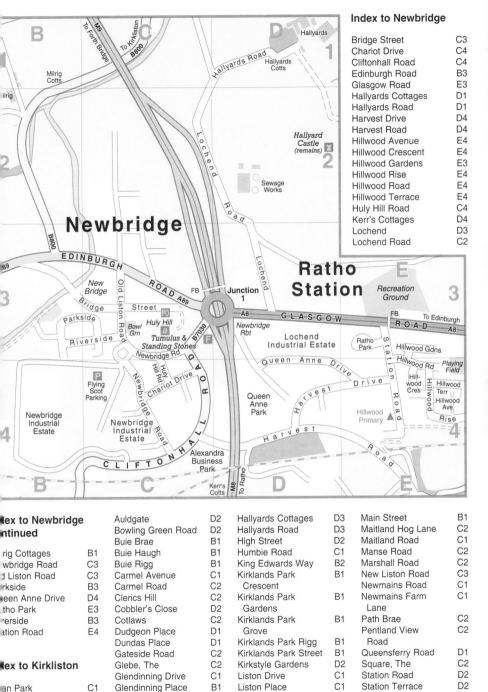

Newbridge

Ratho Station

Index to Newbridge

Bridge Street	C3
Chariot Drive	C4
Cliftonhall Road	C4
Edinburgh Road	B3
Glasgow Road	E3
Hallyards Cottages	D1
Hallyards Road	D1
Harvest Drive	D4
Harvest Road	D4
Hillwood Avenue	E4
Hillwood Crescent	E4
Hillwood Gardens	E3
Hillwood Rise	E4
Hillwood Road	E4
Hillwood Terrace	E4
Huly Hill Road	C4
Kerr's Cottages	D4
Lochend	D3
Lochend Road	C2

Index to Newbridge continued

Milrig Cottages	B1
Newbridge Road	C3
Old Liston Road	C3
Parkside	B3
Queen Anne Drive	D4
Ratho Park	E3
Riverside	B3
Station Road	E4

Index to Kirkliston

...an Park	C1
...son Place	D1
...mondhill Road	D1
...mondside	D2

Auldgate	D2	Hallyards Cottages	D3	Main Street	B1
Bowling Green Road	D2	Hallyards Road	D3	Maitland Hog Lane	C2
Buie Brae	B1	High Street	D2	Maitland Road	C1
Buie Haugh	B1	Humbie Road	C1	Manse Road	C2
Buie Rigg	B1	King Edwards Way	B2	Marshall Road	C2
Carmel Avenue	C1	Kirklands Park	B1	New Liston Road	C3
Carmel Road	C2	Crescent		Newmains Road	C1
Clerics Hill	C2	Kirklands Park	B1	Newmains Farm	C1
Cobbler's Close	D2	Gardens		Lane	
Cotlaws	C2	Kirklands Park	B1	Path Brae	C2
Dudgeon Place	D1	Grove		Pentland View	C2
Dundas Place	D1	Kirklands Park Rigg	B1	Road	
Gateside Road	C2	Kirklands Park Street	B1	Queensferry Road	D1
Glebe, The	C2	Kirkstyle Gardens	D2	Square, The	C2
Glendinning Drive	C1	Liston Drive	C1	Station Road	D2
Glendinning Place	B1	Liston Place	C1	Station Terrace	D2
Glendinning Road	B1	Liston Road	C2	Stewart Place	D1
Glendinning Way	C1	Loanhead Cottages	C1	Toddshill Road	C2
Greigs Hill	C2	Lochend Road	C3	Wellflats Road	D2

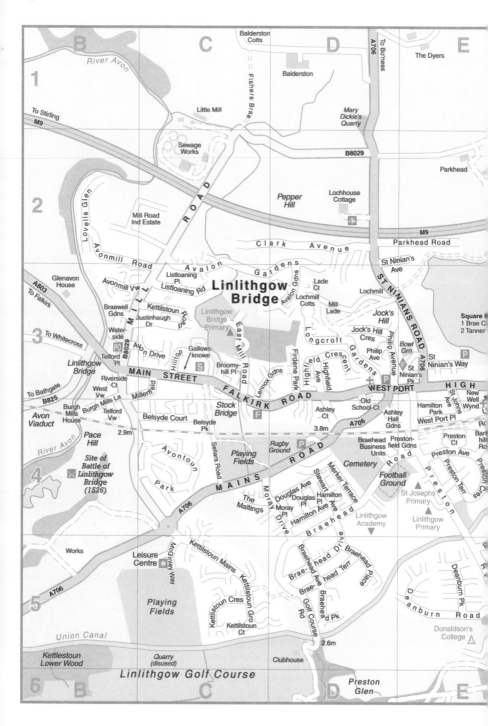

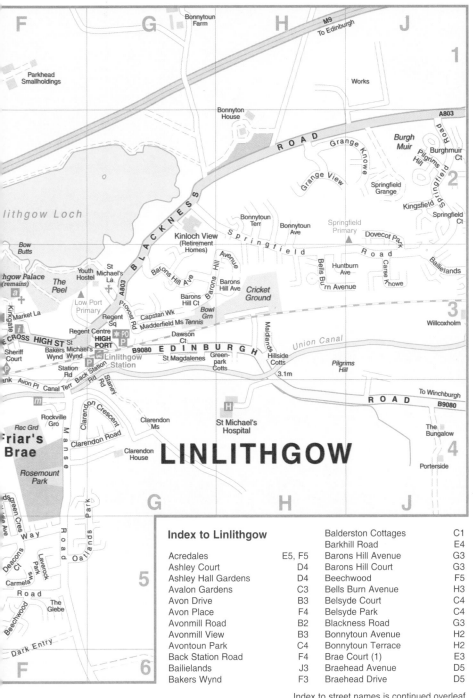

LINLITHGOW

Index to Linlithgow

Acredales	E5, F5
Ashley Court	D4
Ashley Hall Gardens	D4
Avalon Gardens	C3
Avon Drive	B3
Avon Place	F4
Avonmill Road	B2
Avonmill View	B3
Avontoun Park	C4
Back Station Road	F4
Bailielands	J3
Bakers Wynd	F3
Balderston Cottages	C1
Barkhill Road	E4
Barons Hill Avenue	G3
Barons Hill Court	G3
Beechwood	F5
Bells Burn Avenue	H3
Belsyde Court	C4
Belsyde Park	C4
Blackness Road	G3
Bonnytoun Avenue	H2
Bonnytoun Terrace	H2
Brae Court (1)	E3
Braehead Avenue	D5
Braehead Drive	D5

Index to street names is continued overleaf

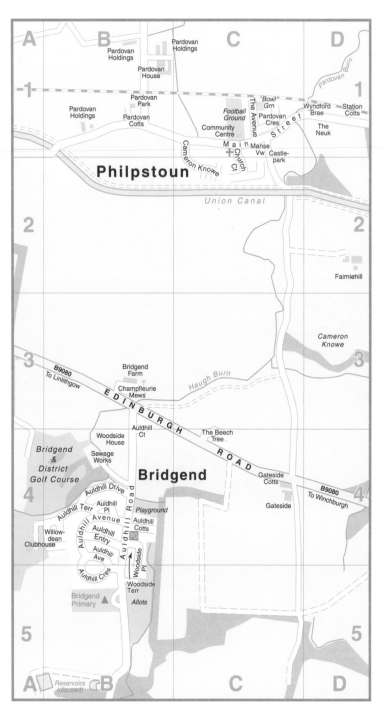

Braehead Park
Braehead Place
Braehead Road
Braehead Terrace
Braewell Gardens
Broomyhill Place
Burgess Hill
Burgh Mills Lane
Burghmuir Court
Canal Terrace
Capstan Walk
Carmelaws
Carse Knowe
Clarendon Crescent
Clarendon Mews
Clarendon Road
Clark Avenue
Cross, The
Dark Entry
Dawson Court
Deacons Court
Deanburn Park
Deanburn Road
Dog Well Wynd
Douglas Avenue
Douglas Place
Dovecot Park
East Mill Road
Edinburgh Road
Falkirk Road
Firdene Park
Fishers Brae
Friars Brae
Friars Loan
Friars Way
Gallowsknowe
Glebe, The
Golf Course Road
Grange Knowe
Grange View
Greenpark Cottages
Hamilton Avenue
Hamilton Park
Hamilton Place
High Port
High Street   E
Highfield Avenue
Highfield Crescent
Hillside Cottages
Hilltop
Huntburn Avenue
Huntingtower Court
Jock's Hill Crescent
Justinhaugh Drive
Kettilstoun Court
Kettilstoun Crescent
Kettilstoun Grove
Kettilstoun Mains
Ketttilstoun Road
Kingsfield
Kirkgate
Lade Court
Laverock Park

x Gardens	C3
Jell Wynd	E3
ning Place	C3
ning Road	C3
ill	D3
ill Cottages	D3
de Mews	E3
roft Gardens	D3
s Glen	B2
ey Way	C5
erfield Mews	G3
nds	H3
Street	B3
Road	C4
gs, The	C4
Road	F4
t Lane	F3
r Terrace	D3
de	D3
ad	B3
eld	B3
Drive	C4
Place	D4
Jell Wynd	E3
ds Park	F5
hool Court	D4
ad Road	D2
Avenue	D3
s Hill	J2
n Avenue	E4
n Court	E4
n Crescent	E4
n Park	E4
n Road	E4
n Terrace	E4
nfield	E4
ens	
Road	E5
st Road	G3
t Square	G3
ton Road	F5
sgreen	F4
ent	
de Court	B3
lle Grove	F4
Terrace	E4
ns Avenue	E3
dalenes	G3
hael's Lane	G3
hael's Wynd	F3
an's Avenue	D5
an's Park	E3
ans Road	D3
an's Way	E3
Road	C4
akers Way	E5
ield Court	J2
field	J2
ge	
ield Road	H2, J2
Road	G4
Road	F3
t Avenue	D4

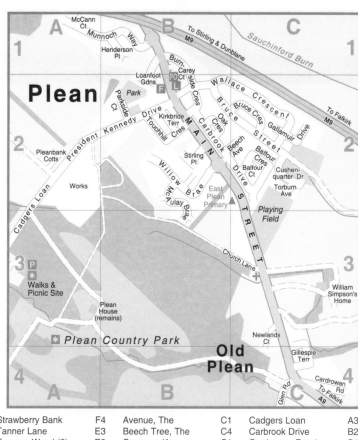

Strawberry Bank	F4
Tanner Lane	E3
Tanners Wynd (2)	E3
Telford Place	B3
Telford View	B4
Union Road	E4
Vennel, The	F3
Waldie Avenue	F4
Waterside	B3
Water Yett	E3
West Port	D3
West Port Place	E4
West View	B3
Whitten Lane	E3

Index to Philpstoun & Bridgend

Auldhill Avenue	B4
Auldhill Cottages	B4
Auldhill Court	B3
Auldhill Crescent	B5
Auldhill Drive	B4
Auldhill Entry	B4
Auldhill Place	B4
Auldhill Road	B4
Auldhill Terrace	B4

Avenue, The	C1
Beech Tree, The	C4
Cameron Knowe	C1
Castlepark	C1
Champfleurie Mews	B3
Church Court	C2
Edinburgh Road	B3
Gateside Cottages	C4
Main Street	C1
Manse View	C1
Neuk , The	D1
Pardovan Cottages	B1
Pardovan Crescent	C1
Station Cottages	D1
Willowdean	B4
Woodside Place	B4
Woodside Terrace	B4
Wyndford Brae	D1

Index to Plean

Balfour Court	C2
Balfour Crescent	C2
Beech Avenue	C2
Bruce Crescent	C2
Bruce Street	B2
Burnside Crescent	B1

Cadgers Loan	A3
Carbrook Drive	B2
Cardrowan Road	C4
Carey Court	B1
Church Lane	C3
Cushenquarter Drive	C2
Gallamuir Drive	C2
Gillespie Terrace	C4
Glen Road	C4
Henderson Place	B1
Kirkbride Terrace	B2
Loanfoot Gardens	B2
McAulay Brae	B2
McCann Court	A1
Main Street	B2
Munnoch Way	A1
Newlands Court	C3
Oak Crescent	B2
Parkside Court	B2
Pleanbank Cottages	A2
President Kennedy Drive	A2
Stirling Place	B2
Torburn Avenue	C2
Touchhill Crescent	B2
Wallace Crescent	C2
Willow Brae	B2

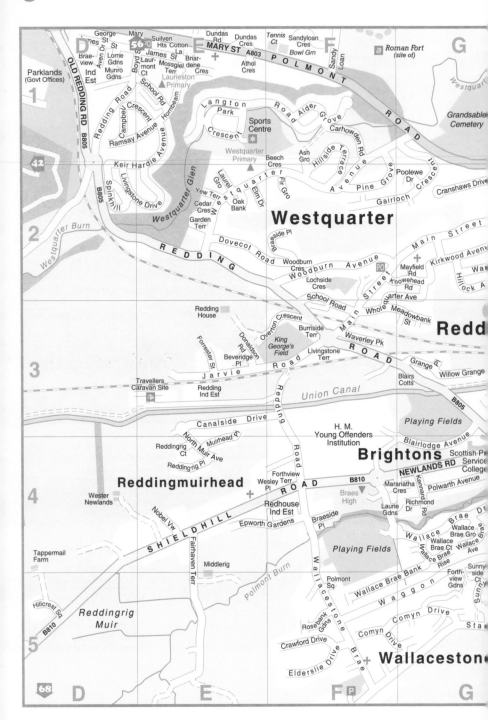

Westquarter

Redd

Reddingmuirhead

Brightons

Wallacestone

Parklands
(Govt Offices)

Roman Fort
(site of)

Grandsable
Cemetery

Sports
Centre

Langton
Park

Westquarter
Primary

Lauriestion
Primary

Westquarter Glen

Westquarter Burn

Redding
House

King
George's
Field

Travellers
Caravan Site

Redding
Ind Est

Union Canal

H. M.
Young Offenders
Institution

Playing Fields

Scottish P
Service
College

Redhouse
Ind Est

Braes
High

Wester
Newlands

Tappermail
Farm

Reddingrig
Muir

Playing Fields

Polmont
Sq

Wallacestone Brae

Polmont Burn

OLD REDDING RD

B805

MARY ST A803

POLMONT ROAD

REDDING ROAD

SHIELDHILL

NEWLANDS RD

B810

B805

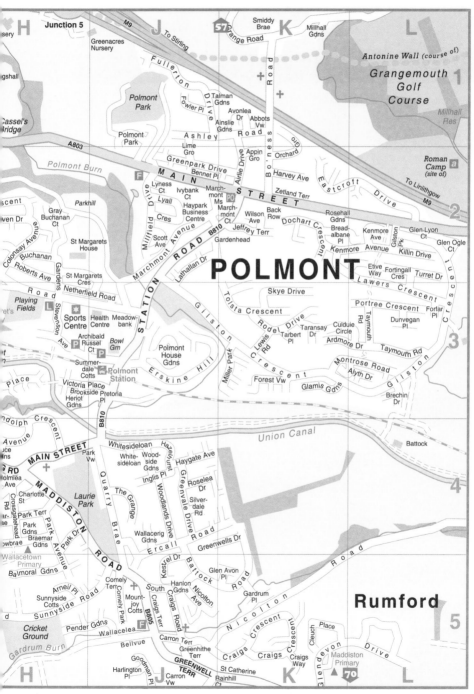

Junction 5

Greenacres Nursery

M9

To Stirling

Smiddy Brae

Grange Road

Millhall Gdns

Antonine Wall *(course of)*

Grangemouth Golf Course

Millhall Res

Fullerton Drive

Polmont Park

Fowler Pl

Talman Gdns

Avonlea Dr

Abbots Vw.

Orchard

Roman Camp *(site of)*

To Linlithgow

M9

Ainslie Gdns

Ashley Road

Appin Gro

Harvey Ave

Eastcroft Drive

Cassel's Bridge

A803

Polmont Park

Lime Gro

Greenpark Drive

Bennet Pl

MAIN

Airlie Drive

Boness Gro

Zetland Terr

Polmont Burn

Parkhill

Lyness Ct

Ivybank Ct

Marchmont Ms

STREET

Wilson Ave

Back Row

Rosehall Gdns

Gray Buchanan Ct

Lyall Cres

Haypark Business Centre

Marchmont Ct

Jeffrey Terr

Dochart Crescent

Breadalbane Pl

Kenmore Ave

Gillston Pk

Glen Lyon Ct

Glen Ogle Ct

St Margarets House

Scott Ave

Gardenhead

Kenmore Avenue

Killin Drive

Colonsay Ave

Buchanan Gardens

St Margarets Cres

Marchmont Avenue

STATION ROAD

B810

Lathallan Dr

POLMONT

Etive Way

Fortingall Cres

Turret Dr

Roberts Ave

Netherfield Road

Millfield Drive

Skye Drive

Lawers Crescent

Playing Fields

Stevenson Ave

Sports Centre

Health Centre

Meadowbank

Tolsta Crescent

Rodel Drive

Portree Crescent

Forfar Pl

Gillston Crescent

Taymouth Cres

Dunvegan Pl

Archibald Russel Ct

Bowl Grn

Polmont House Gdns

Gilston Hill

Tarbert Pl

Taransay Dr

Culduie Circle

Ardmore Dr

Taymouth Rd

Summerdale Cotts

Polmont Station

Erskine Hill

Miller Park

Lewis Rd

Crescent

Montrose Road

Alyth Dr

Gilston

Victoria Place

Brookside

Pretoria Pl

Heriot Gdns

Forest Vw

Glamis Gdns

Brechin Dr

Randolph Crescent

Union Canal

Battock

Avenue

Bruce Gdns

MAIN STREET

Whitesideloan

Hazelhurst

Park Vw

Whitesideloan

Woodside Gdns

Haygate Ave

RD

Holmlea Ave

MADDISTON ROAD

Inglis Pl

Greenvale Drive

Roselea Dr

Charlotte St

Laurie Park

The Grange

Woodlands Drive

Silverdale Rd

Crossgatehead Rd

Park Terr

Park Gdns

Braemar Gdns

Park Avenue

Quarry Brae

Wallacerig Gdns

Road

Greenwells Dr

Ercall

Wallacetown Primary

Balmoral Gdns

Kesel Dr

Battock Crescent

Glen Avon Pl

Road

Nicolton Road

Arneil Pl

Sunnyside Cotts

Comely Terr

Mountjoy Cotts

Hanlon Gdns

Nicolton Ave

Gardrum Pl

Rumford

Sunnyside Road

South Craigs Terr

Craigs Road

Cricket Ground

Pender Gdns

Comely Park

B805

Nicolton Crescent

Place

Glendevon Drive

Gardrum Burn

Wallacelea

Bellvue

Carron Terr

Greenhithe Terr

Craigs

Craigs

Craigs Crescent

Cleuch

Craigs Way

Maddiston Primary

70

Harlington Pl

Goodman Pl

GREENWELL TERR

Carron Vw

St Catherine

Rainhill Ct

Index to street names can be found overleaf

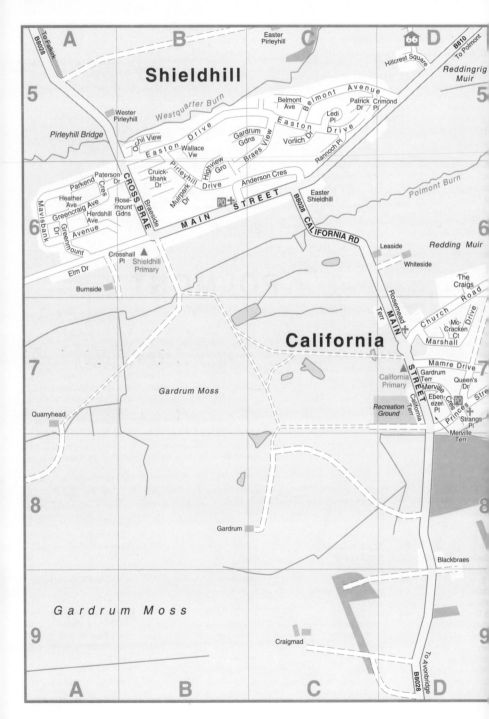

Shieldhill

California

ex to Polmont, California, Shieldhill, Maddiston & Rumford

ts View	K1	Canalside Drive	E3	Fowler Crescent	L7	James Street	D1
cairney Crescent	J6	Carhowden Road	F1	Fowler Place	J1	James Wilson Drive	L7
Court	K6	Carron Terrace	J5	Fullerton Drive	J1	Jarvie Road	E3
e Gardens	K1	Carron View	J5	Gairloch Crescent	F2	Jeffrey Terrace	K2
Drive	K2	Cedar Crescent	E2	Garden Terrace	E2	Keir Hardie Avenue	D1
Grove	F1	Charlotte Street	H4	Gardenhead	K2	Kendieshill Avenue	L7
Drive	L3	Chrisella Terrace	L6	Gardrum Gardens	B5	Kenmore Avenue	L2
rson Crescent	C6	Church Road	D7	Gardrum Place	K5	Kennard Road	G4
rson Gardens	J6	Cleuch Place	K5	Gardrum Terrace	D7	Kestrel Drive	J5
Grove	K2	Colonsay Avenue	H2	George Street	D1	Killin Drive	L2
bald Russell	H3	Comely Park	J5	Gilston Crescent	L3, J3	Kirkwood Avenue	G2
rt		Comely Terrace	J5	Gilston Park	L2	Knowehead Road	F2
ore Drive	L3	Comyn Drive	G5	Glamis Gardens	K3	Langton Road	E1
l Place	H5	Cotton Lane	E1	Glendale	J4	Lathallan Drive	J2
Grove	F1	Craigend Drive	L6	Glendevon Drive	K5	Laurel Grove	E2
y Road	J1	Craiglaw Terrace	H4	Glen Avon Place	K5	Laurie Gardens	F4
Crescent	E1	Craigs Crescent	K5	Glen Lyon Court	L2	Laurmont Court	E1
Drive	D1	Craigs Terrace	J5	Glen Ogle Court	L2	Lawers Crescent	L2
ea Drive	K1	Craigs Way	K5	Goodman Place	J5	Lawson Place	L7
Drive	L3	Craigs, The	D6	Grandsable Road	G1	Ledi Place	C5
Row	K2	Cranshaws Drive	G2	Grange Place	G3	Ledmore Place	B3
oral Gardens	H5	Crawford Drive	F5	Grange Road	K1	Lewis Road	K3
ck Road	J5	Cricket Place	G3	Grange, The	J4	Lime Grove	J1
cross Road	F2	Crimond Place	C5	Gray Buchanan Court	H2	Livingstone Drive	D2
h Crescent	F1	Cross Brae	B6	Greencraig Avenue	A6	Livingstone Terrace	F3
vue	J5	Crossgatehead	H4	Greenhithe Terrace	J5	Lochside Crescent	F2
ont Avenue	C5	Road		Greenmount Drive	A6	Lorne Gardens	D1
et Place	J2	Crosshall Place	B6	Greenpark Drive	J2	Lyall Crescent	J2
esda Grove	J6	Cruickshank Drive	B6	Greens, The	J6	Lyness Court	J2
ridge Place	E3	Culquie Circle	K3	Greenvale Drive	J4	McCracken Court	D7
mount Terrace	J6	Dochart Crescent	K2	Greenwell Terrace	J5	MacArthur Crescent	J6
odge Avenue	G4	Donaldson Road	E3	Greenwells Drive	J4	Maddiston Road	H4
Cottages	G3	Douglas Avenue	H4	Haining Grove	M7	Main Street	H4
ess Road	K2	Dovecot Road	E2	Haining, The	M5	(Brightons)	
on Road	J9	Dundas Crescent	E1	Hamilton Crescent	J6	Main Street	D7
Street	E1	Dundas Road	E1	Hanlon Gardens	J5	(California)	
nar Gardens	H4	Dunvegan Place	L3	Harlington Place	J5	Main Street	L6
s View	C5	Eastcroft Drive	L2	Harlow Avenue	G3	(Maddiston)	
side	B6	Easton Drive	B5, C5	Harvey Avenue	K2	Main Street	J2
side Place	F3	Ebenezer Place	D7	Haygate Avenue	J4	(Polmont)	
dding)		Eccles Place	L7	Hazelhurst	J4	Main Street	F3
side Place	F4	Elderslie Drive	F5	Heather Avenue	A6	(Redding)	
ddingmuirhead)		Elm Drive (Shieldhill)	A6	Heather Grove	L7	Main Street	B6
s View	B5	Elm Drive (Redding)	E2	Herdshill Avenue	A6	(Shieldhill)	
view	D1	Epworth Gardens	E4	Heriot Gardens	H3	Mamre Drive	D7
albane Place	K2	Ercall Road	J4	High Road	L7	Manor Wynd	L6
in Drive	L3	Erskine Hill	J3	Highview Grove	B6	Manuel Rigg	J6
Brae	H4	Etive Way	L2	Hillcrest Square	D5	Maranatha Crescent	F4
ene	E1	Fairhaven Terrace	E4	Hillock Avenue	G2	Marchmont Avenue	J2
side	H3	Fairways Avenue	K6	Hillside Terrace	F1	Marchmont Court	K2
Gardens	H4	Fir Grove	F2	Hillview Road	H4	Marshall Drive	D7
anan Gardens	H2	Forest View	K3	Holmlea Avenue	H4	Marchmont Mews	K2
side Terrace	F3	Forfar Place	L3	Hornbeam Crescent	E1	Mary Square	D1
eymount Avenue	L6	Forgie Crescent	L7	Inglis Place	J4	Mary Street	E1
rnia Road	J6	Forrester Street	E3	Ingram Place	J6	Mavisbank Avenue	A6
rnia Terrace	D7	Forthview Gardens	G5	Ivybank Court	J2	Mayfield Road	G2
bell Crescent	D1	Forthview Terrace	F4	James Smith	J6	Meadowbank	J3
l Walk	G3	Fortingall Crescent	L2	Avenue		Meadowbank Street	G3

Index to street names is continued overleaf

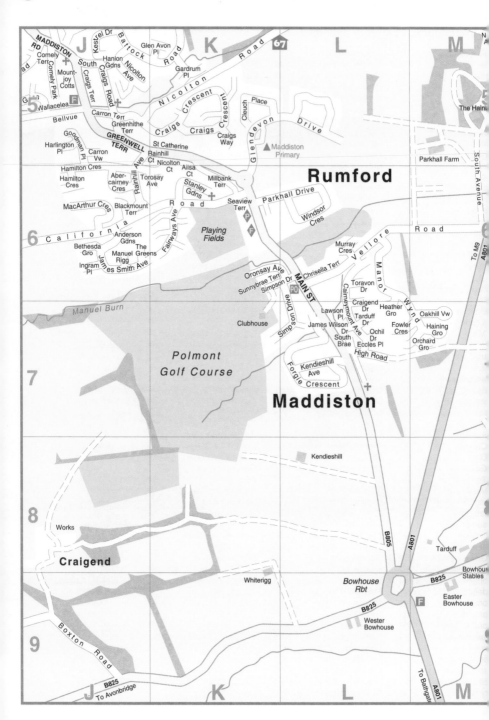

Rumford

Maddiston

Polmont Golf Course

Craigend

Works

Whiterigg

Kendieshill

Bowhouse Rbt

Wester Bowhouse

Easter Bowhouse

Bowhouse Stables

Tarduff

The Haini

Parkhall Farm

Maddiston Primary

x to Polmont, California, Shieldhill, Maddiston & Rumford continued

lle Crescent	D7	Queen's Drive	D7	Talman Gardens	K1
lle Terrace	D7	Rainhill Avenue	J6	Taransay Drive	K3
nk Terrace	K6	Rainhill Court	K5	Tarbert Place	K3
Park	K3	Ramsay Avenue	D1	Tarduff Drive	L7
ld Drive	J2	Randolph Crescent	H4	Taymouth Road	L3
ll Gardens	K1	Rannoch Place	C5	Tiree Crescent	H2
ose Road	L3	Redding Road	D1, F3	Tolsta Crescent	K3
en Drive	H2	Reddingrig Court	E4	Toravon Drive	L6
tjoy Cottages	J5	Reddingrig Place	E4	Torosay Avenue	K6
giel Terrace	E1	Richmond Drive	G4	Tudor Court	G2
ead Place	E4	Roberts Avenue	H2	Turret Drive	L2
ark Drive	B6	Rodel Drive	K3	Union Place	H3
o Gardens	D1	Rosebank Gardens	F5	Vellore Road	L6
y Crescent	L6	Roselea Drive	J4	Victoria Place	H3
rfield Road	H3	Rosehall Gardens	K2	Vorlich Drive	C5
ands Road	G4	Rosemead Terrace	D7	Waggon Road	F5
on Avenue	J5	Rosemount Gardens	B6	Wallace Brae	G4
on Court	K5	St Catherine	K5	Avenue	
on Road	K5	St Margaret's	H2	Wallace Brae Bank	F5
l View	E4	Crescent		Wallace Brae Court	G4
Avenue	M5	St Margaret's	H3	Wallace Brae Drive	G4
Muir Avenue	E4	Gardens		Wallace Brae	G4
Bank	E2	Salmon Inn Park	G2	Gardens	
ill View	M7	Salmon Inn Road	H2	Wallace Brae Grove	G4
Drive	L7	Sandy Loan	F1	Wallace Brae Rise	G4
View	B5	Sandyloan Crescent	F1	Wallace Crescent	G4
edding Road	D1	School Road	E1	Wallace View	B5
ard Grove	M7	(Laurieston)		Wallacelea	J5
ddiston)		School Road	F2	Wallacerig Gardens	J4
ard Grove	K2	(Redding)		Wallacestone Brae	F4
mont)		School View	G3	Ward Avenue	G2
ard, The	H4	Scott Avenue	J2	Waverley Park	F3
say Avenue	K6	Seaview Terrace	K6	Wesley Place	E4
on Crescent	E3	Shieldhill Road	E4	Westquarter Avenue	E2
Avenue	H4	Silverdale Road	J4	Whitesideloan	J4
Crescent	E1	Simpson Drive	L6	Wholequarter Avenue	F3
Drive	H4	Skye Drive	K3	Willowbrae	H4
Gardens	H4	South Avenue	M5	Willow Grange	G3
Terrace	H4	South Brae (2)	L7	Wilson Avenue	K2
View	J4	South Craigs	J5	Windsor Crescent	L6
nd Crescent	A6	Road		Woodburn Avenue	F2
all Drive	K6	Spinkhill	D2	Woodburn Crescent	F2
son Drive	A6	Station Road	J3	Woodlands Drive	J4
k Drive	C5	Standrigg Avenue	G5	Woodside Gardens	J4
er Gardens	H5	Standrigg Gardens	H5	Yew Terrace	E2
Grove	F2	Standrigg Road	G5	Zetland Terrace	K2
hill Drive	B5	Stanley Gardens	K6		
ont House	J3	Stevenson Avenue	H3		
dens		Strangs Place	D7		
ont Park	J1	Suilven Heights	E1		
ont Road	F1	Summerdale	J3		
ont Square	F5	Cottages			
arth Avenue	G4	Sunnybrae Terrace	K6		
we Drive	G2	Sunnyside Avenue	G5		
ee Crescent	L3	Sunnyside Cottages	H5		
ria Place	J3	Sunnyside Court	G5		
es Street	D7	Sunnyside Drive	G5		
y Brae	J4	Sunnyside Road	H5		

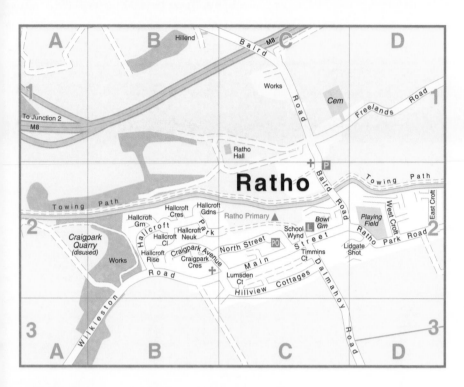

Index to Ratho

Baird Road	C1, C2
Craigpark Avenue	B2
Craigpark Crescent	B2
Dalmahoy Road	C2
East Croft	D2
Freelands Road	D1
Hallcroft Close	B2
Hallcroft Crescent	B2
Hallcroft Gardens	B2
Hallcroft Green	B2
Hallcroft Neuk	B2
Hallcroft Park	B2
Hallcroft Rise	B2
Hillview Cottages	C2
Lidgate Shot	D2
Lumsden Court	C2
Main Street	C2
North Street	C2
Ratho Park Road	D2
School Wynd	C2
Timmins Court	C2
West Croft	D2
Wilkieston Road	B3

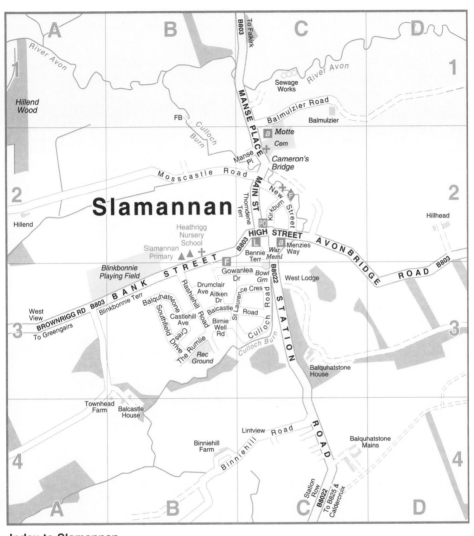

Index to Slamannan

Aitken Drive	B3
Avonbridge Road	C2
Balcastle Road	B3
Balmulzier Road	C1
Balquhatstone Crescent	B3
Bank Street	B3
Bennie Terrace	C2
Binniehill Road	B4
Birniewell Road	B3
Blinkbonnie Terrace	A3
Brownrigg Road	A3
Castlehill Avenue	B3
Culloch Road	C3
Drumclair Avenue	B3
Gowanlea Drive	B3
High Street	C2
Kirkburn	C2
Lintview	C4
Main Street	C2
Manse Place	C1, C2
Menzies Way	C2
Mosscastle Road	B2
New Street	C2
Rashiehill Road	B3
Rumlie, The	B3
St Laurence Crescent	B3
Southfield Drive	B3
Station Road	C3
Thorndene Terrace	C2

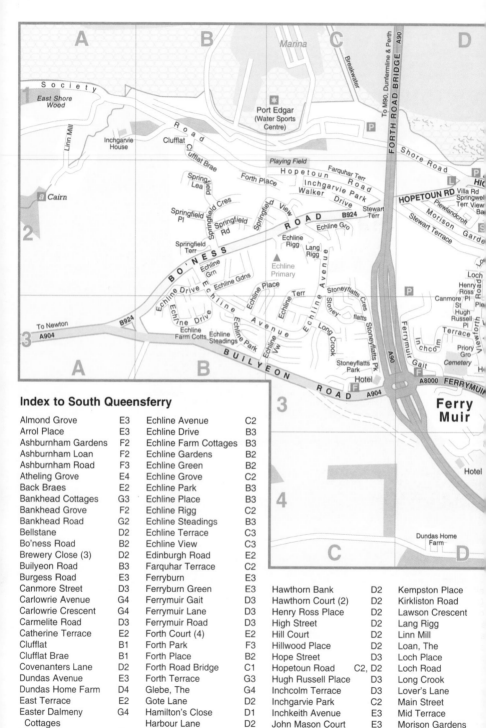

Index to South Queensferry

Almond Grove	E3	Echline Avenue	C2			
Arrol Place	E3	Echline Drive	B3			
Ashburnham Gardens	F2	Echline Farm Cottages	B3			
Ashburnham Loan	F2	Echline Gardens	B2			
Ashburnham Road	F3	Echline Green	B2			
Atheling Grove	E4	Echline Grove	C2			
Back Braes	E2	Echline Park	B3			
Bankhead Cottages	G3	Echline Place	B3			
Bankhead Grove	F2	Echline Rigg	C2			
Bankhead Road	G2	Echline Steadings	B3			
Bellstane	D2	Echline Terrace	C3			
Bo'ness Road	B2	Echline View	C3			
Brewery Close (3)	D2	Edinburgh Road	E2			
Builyeon Road	B3	Farquhar Terrace	C2			
Burgess Road	E3	Ferryburn	E3			
Canmore Street	D3	Ferryburn Green	E3	Hawthorn Bank	D2	Kempston Place	
Carlowrie Avenue	G4	Ferrymuir Gait	D3	Hawthorn Court (2)	D2	Kirkliston Road	
Carlowrie Crescent	G4	Ferrymuir Lane	D3	Henry Ross Place	D2	Lawson Crescent	
Carmelite Road	D3	Ferrymuir Road	D3	High Street	D2	Lang Rigg	
Catherine Terrace	E2	Forth Court (4)	E2	Hill Court	D2	Linn Mill	
Clufflat	B1	Forth Park	F3	Hillwood Place	D2	Loan, The	
Clufflat Brae	B1	Forth Place	B2	Hope Street	D3	Loch Place	
Covenanters Lane	D2	Forth Road Bridge	C1	Hopetoun Road	C2, D2	Loch Road	
Dundas Avenue	E3	Forth Terrace	G3	Hugh Russell Place	D3	Long Crook	
Dundas Home Farm	D4	Glebe, The	G4	Inchcolm Terrace	D3	Lover's Lane	
East Terrace	E2	Gote Lane	D2	Inchgarvie Park	C2	Main Street	
Easter Dalmeny	G4	Hamilton's Close	D1	Inchkeith Avenue	E3	Mid Terrace	
Cottages		Harbour Lane	D2	John Mason Court	E3	Morison Gardens	
Echline	B3	Hawes Brae	F2	Kempston Grove	E3	Moubray Grove	

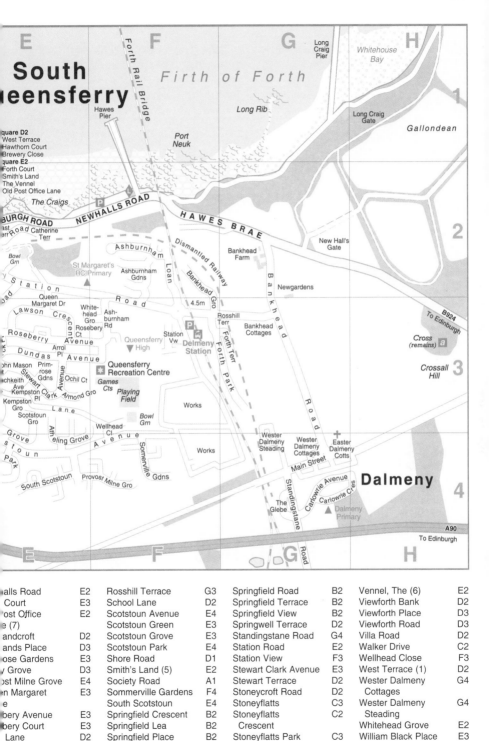

STIRLING

Cornton

Kildean

Raploch

Junction 10

Cornton Vale HM Prison
Cornton Vale Cotts
To Bridge of Allan
Castle Vale
Cornton Primary
De Moray Ct
Westhaugh Rd
John Cowane Row
Ben Lomond Dr
Sunnyside Pl
Old Bridge Wynd
Harvest St
River Wynd
Westhaugh Road
Waterfront Way
Ferry Ct
Fleurs Park
Borrows Gate
Fishermans Wk

Old Mills Farm
The Weir Bungalow

Road
John Rushforth Pl
Woodside Rd
Hawthorn Cres
Hazelbank
Thistle Pl
Ivanhoe Place Gardens
Beatty Avenue
Menzies Drive
Duncan Ct
Mosspiel Ave
Ken Burns St
Balfour St
Ferguson St
Stewart Sq
MacPherson Dr
Winchel Pl
Gordon Sq
Fisher Row
RAPLOCH ROAD
Raploch Community Campus
Castleview School
Raploch Prim
Our Lady's Primary
S

Carseview House
Bremner House
Robertson House
The Castle Business Park
Kildean Hospital
DRIP
Weir Street
O'Hanlon Way
B8051
Argyll Ct
Scotia House
Strathallan House
Erskine Ct
Maxxium House
Glendevon House
Bermuda House
Lomond Ct
King Robert Ct
Craighall St
Waulker Ave
Cordiner Cl
Atholl Pl
Huntly Cl
Crescent
Hope St
Glendevon Drive
RAPLOCH
Craigforth Cres
Craigforth Crescent
Elm St
Oak St
Duff Cres
Gowanhill Gdns
Back o'Hill Road
Raploch
Football Pitch
Back o'Hill Industrial Estate
Back o' Hill Road
Ballengeich Road

River Forth

M9
To Forth
A84
A84
M9
M9

Falleninch

To Edinburgh
To Gargunnock
A811

Millennium Way

ROAD
B8051

DUMBARTON ROAD
A811

Square E5
1 Mar Place
2 Jail Wynd

King's Park Farm

Royal Gardens
King's Knot

Gowan Hill
Cemetery
Ballengeich Pass
Ballengeich Walk
Stirling Castle
Lower Castlehill
Upper Castlehill
Visitor Centre
Esplanade
Argyll's Lodging
Mar's Wark
Church of The Holy Rude
Royal Gdns
Guildhall
Old Town
Smith Art Gallery & Museum

The Beheading Stone
Crofthead Ct
Castle Ct
Kings Stables La
Castle Wynd
Kelly Ct
Broad St
Bowl Gm
YH

Cornton Primary
Cornton
River

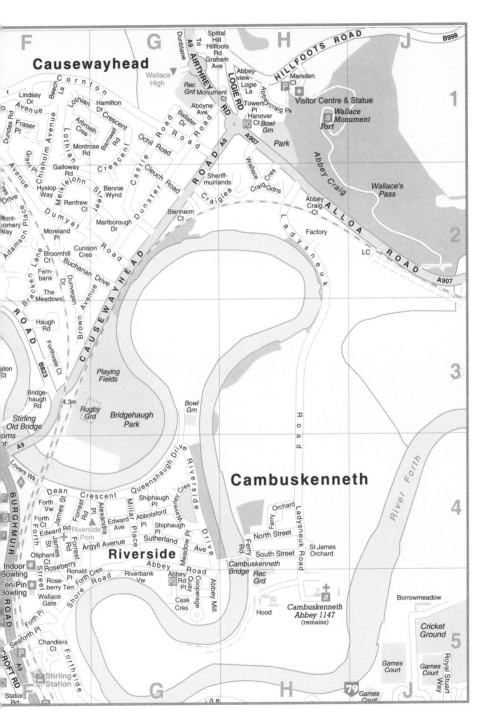

Causewayhead

B998

HILLFOOTS ROAD

Spittal Hill
Hillfoots Rd
Graham Ave
Durblane
To
AIRTHREY
A9
Wallace High
Rec Grd
Abboyne Ave
Balater Dr
LOGIE RD
Abbey view
Logie La
Marsden Ct
Abbeycraig Pk
Visitor Centre & Statue
Wallace Monument
Towers Pl
Hanover Ct
Bowl Gm
Fort
Wallace High
Monument

Cornton
Lindsay Dr
Beech La
Lothian Avenue
Hamilton Dr
Arbroath Cres
Montrose Rd
Galloway Rd
Ochil Road
Castle Road
Cleuch Road
Crescent
Bennie Wynd
Sheriff-muirlands
Wallace Cres
Craig Gdns
Park
A907

Fraser Pl
Dundas Pl
Grant Avenue
Chisholm Avenue
Lothian
Meiklejohn
Hyslop Way
Renfrew Ct
Dumyat Road
Marlborough Dr
Craiglea
Blenheim Ct
Abbey Craig Ct
ALLOA ROAD
Wallace's Pass

Drive
Mont- gomery Way
Adamson
Place
Moreland Pl
Cunison Cres
Dunster Road
Factory
LC
A907

Bracken Lane
Fern- bank
The Meadows
Buchanan Drive
Dunvegan
Brown Avenue
Ladysneuk
Abbey Craig

ROAD
Haugh Rd
CAUSEWAYHEAD
ROAD

B823
Forthvale Ct
Playing Fields

Bridge- haugh Rd
4.3m
Rugby Grd
Bridgehaugh Park
Bowl Grn
Road

Stirling Old Bridge
oms
A9

Lovers Wk

BURGHMUIR
Queenshaugh Drive
Riverside Drive
Cambuskenneth
River Forth

Dean Crescent
Shiphaugh Pl
Waverley Cres
Orchard
Ladysneuk Road

Forth Vw
Forth Ct
Forest Pl
Alexandra
Millar Pl
Edward Ave
Abbotsford Pl
Shiphaugh Pl
North Street
Ferry Rd
St James Orchard

St James St
Forth St
James St
Edward Rd
Riverside Prim
Argyll Avenue
Sutherland
Abbey Ave
South Street
Cambuskenneth Bridge
Rec Grd

Oliphant Ct
Forrest Rd
Roseberry
Ronald Pl
Abbey Road
Abbey Rd Pl

Indoor Bowling
Ten-Pin Bowling
Rose- berry Terr
Forth Cres
Riverbank Vw
Riverside
Abbey Quay
Cooperage

ROAD
Wallace Gate
Shore Road
Cask Cres
Abbey Mill
Hood
Cambuskenneth Abbey 1147 (remains)
Borrowmeadow

Seaforth Pl
Chandlers Ct
Forthside
Cricket Ground

P
Stirling Station
Games Court
Games Court
Royal Stuart Way

CROFT RD
A9
Station Rd
79
Games Court

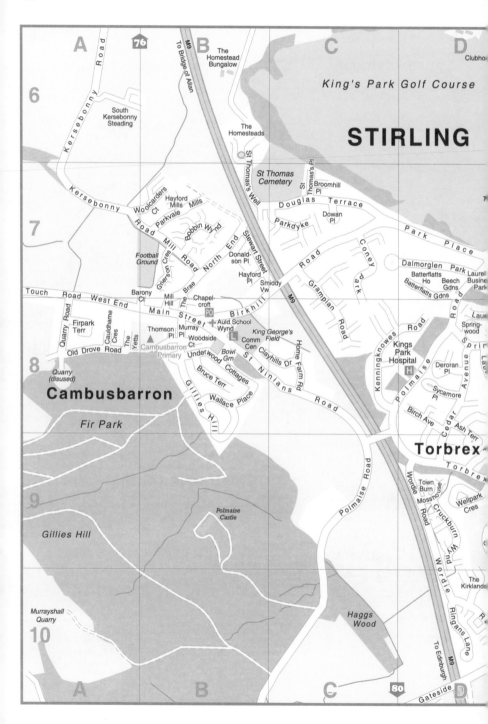

King's Park Golf Course

STIRLING

Clubho

St Thomas Cemetery

St Thomas's Well
St Thomas's Pl
Broomhill Pl

Douglas Terrace

Dowan Pl

Parkdyke

Park Place

The Homestead Bungalow

The Homesteads

76
To Bridge of Allan
M9

Kersebonny Road
South Kersebonny Steading

Kersebonny

Kersebonny Road

Woolcarders Ct
Hayford Mills
Parvale Mills
Parkvale

Bobbin Wynd

Football Ground

Gnerson Cres
Mill Road
North End
The Brae
Stewart Street

Donaldson Pl
Hayford Pl
Smiddy Vw

Coney Park
Road
Grampian Road

Dalmorglen Park
Batterflatts Ho
Beech Gdns
Batterflatts Gdns
Laurel Busine Park

Touch Road
West End
Main Street

Barony Ct
Mill Hill
Chapel-croft
PO
Birkhill
Auld School Wynd

King George's Field
Comm Cen
Clayhills Dr

Home Farm Rd

Laur
Springwood

Road
Road
Spri

Quarry Road
Firpark Terr
Cauldhame Cres
Old Drove Road
The Yetts

Thomson Pl
Murray Pl
Woodside Ct
Cambusbarron Primary
Underwood Cottages
Bowl Grn
St Ninians Road

Kings Park Hospital
H

Kenningknowes Road
Polmaise Road

Deroran Pl
Sycamore Pl
Birch Ave

Cedar Ash Terr
Avenue

Quarry (disused)

Cambusbarron

Bruce Terr
Wallace Place

Gillies Hill

Torbrex

Torbrex

Fir Park

Polmaise Castle

Gillies Hill

Polmaise Road

Town Burn
Mossneuk
Wordie Road
Cruckburn Wynd

Wellpark Cres

Wordie Road
Ringans Lane
The Kirklands

Murrayshall Quarry

Haggs Wood

To Edinburgh
M9

80
Gateside

A   B   C   D

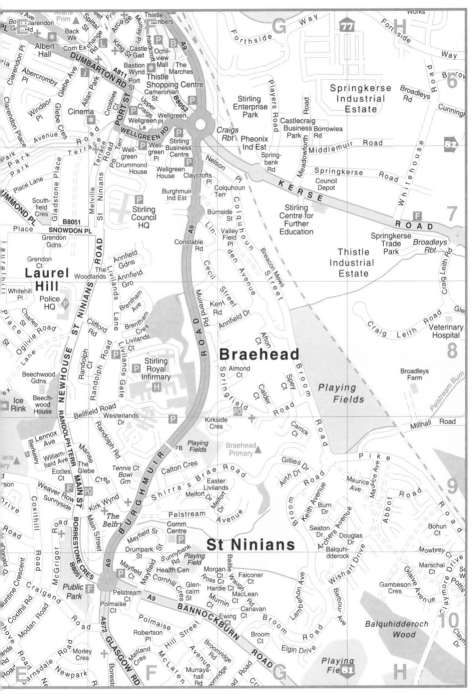

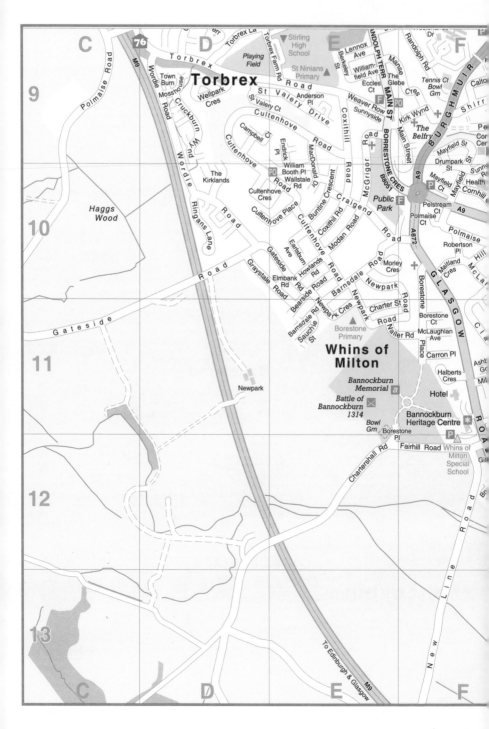

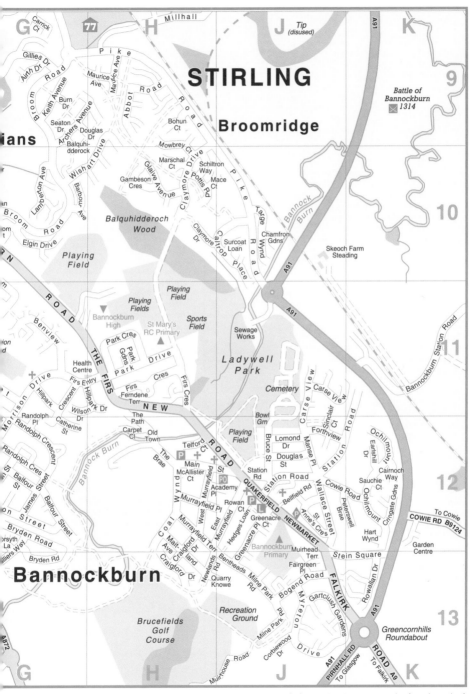

Index to street names can be found overleaf

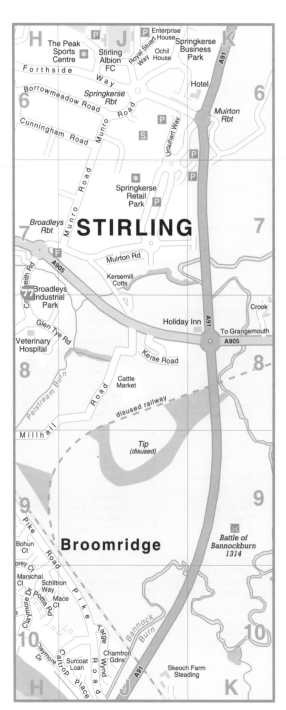

Index to Stirling

Abbey Craig Court	H2
Abbey Mill	G5
Abbey Road Place	G5
Abbey Road	G4
Abbeycraig Park	H1
Abbeyview	H1
Abbot Road	H9
Abbotsford Place	G4
Abercromby Place	E6
Aboyne Avenue	G1
Academy Place	H12
Academy Road	E5
Achray Drive	E2
Adamson Place	F2
Afton Court	G8
Airth Drive	G9
Airthrey Road	G1
Aitken Crescent	F11
Albert Place	E6
Alexandra Place	G4
Allan Park	F6
Alloa Road	J2
Almond Court	G8
Anderson Place	E9
Annfield Drive	G8
Annfield Gardens	F7
Annfield Grove	F7
Arbroath Crescent	F1
Arcade	F6
Archers Avenue	G9
Argyll Avenue	G4
Argyll Court	C3
Ash Terrace	D8
Ashbrae Gardens	F11
Atholl Place	D3
Auld School Wynd	B8
Back o'Hill Road	D4
Back Walk	D5
Baillie Waugh Road	G10
Baker Street	E5
Balfour Street (Kildean)	D3
Balfour Street (Bannockburn)	G12
Ballater Drive	G1
Ballengeich Pass	E4
Ballengeich Road	D4
Balmoral Place	D6
Balquhidderock	G9
Bank Street	E5
Bannockburn Road	F10
Bannockburn Station Road	K11
Barbour Avenue	G10
Barn Road	E5
Barnsdale Road	E10
Barnton Street	F5
Barnwell Road	G1
Barony Court	B8
Bastion Wynd	F6
Batterflatts Gardens	D7
Batterflatts House	
Bayne Street	
Bearside Road	
Beaton Avenue	
Beatty Avenue	
Beech Gardens	
Beech Lane	
Beechwood Gardens	
Bellfield Road (Stirling)	
Bellfield Road (Bannockburn)	
Ben Lomond Drive	
Bennie Wynd	
Bentheads	
Benview	
Berkeley Street	
Bermuda House	
Birch Avenue	
Birkhill Road	
Blenheim Court	
Bobbin Wynd	
Bogend Road	
Bohun Court	
Borestone Court	
Borestone Crescent	
Borestone Place	
Borrowlea Road	
Borrowmeadow Road	
Borrows Gate	
Bow Street	
Bracken Lane	
Brae, The (Cambusbarron)	
Brae, The (Bannockburn)	
Braehead Road	
Breacon Mews	
Bremner House	
Brentham Avenue	
Brentham Crescent	
Bridgehaugh Road	
Broad Street	
Broadleys Road	
Brock Place	
Broom Court	
Broom Road	G8
Broomhill Court	
Broomhill Place	
Broomridge Road	
Brown Avenue	
Bruce Street (Stirling)	
Bruce Street (Bannockburn)	
Bruce Terrace	
Bruce View	
Bryden Road	
Buchanan Drive	
Buntine Crescent	
Burghmuir Road	F

Drive	G9	Craiglea	G2	Falkirk Road	J13	Haugh Road	F3
Street	E3	Cringate Gardens	K12	Ferguson Street	D3	Hawthorn Crescent	D3
de Street	G7	Crofthead Court	E4	Fernbank	F2	Hayford Mills	B7
ch Way	K12	Crofthead Road	E4	Ferndene Terrace	H11	Hayford Place	B7
Court	G8	Crosbies Court	F6	Ferry Court	E2	Hazelbank Gardens	E3
Crescent	F9	Cruachan Avenue	F2	Ferry Orchard	H4	Hedges Loan	J12
Place	J10	Cruckburn Wynd	D9	Ferry Road	H4	Hill Street	F10
ronian Street	F6	Crum Crescent	G10	Firpark Terrace	A8	Hillfoots Road	G1, H1
bell Court	D9	Cultenhove Crescent	D10	Firs Crescent	H11	Hillpark Crescent	G11
an Court	G10	Cultenhove Place	D10	Firs Entry	G11	Hillpark Drive	H11
Close	H12	Cultenhove Road	E10	Firs, The	H11	Hillside House	D7
k Court	G9	Cunison Crescent	F2	Fisher Row	D3	Home Farm Road	C8
Place	F11	Cunningham Road	H6	Fishermans Walk	E2	Hope Street	D4
View	J11	Dalgleish Court	F5	Fleurs Park	D2	Howlands Road	E10
view House	C3	Dalmorglen Park	D7	Forrest Road	F4	Huntly Crescent	D3
Crescent	G5	Darnley Street	E5	Forsyth Lane	G12	Hyslop Way	F2
Court	E5	Davidson Street	G12	Forth Court	F4	Irvine Place	E5
Gait	F6	Dean Crescent	F4	Forth Crescent	F5	Ivanhoe Place	E3
Road	G2	De Moray Court	E1	Forth Place	F5	Jail Wynd (2)	E5
Vale	D1	Deroran Place	D8	Forth Street	F4	James Street	F4
Wynd	E5	Devlin Court	F12	Forth View	F4	(Stirling)	
rine Street	G12	Donaldson Place	B7	Forthside Way	F5, G6, H6	James Street	G12
hame Crescent	A8	Douglas Drive	H9	Forthvale Court	F3	(Bannockburn)	
wayhead Road	G3	Douglas Street	F4	Forthview	J12	John Cowane Row	E1
Street	F7	(Stirling)		Fraser Place	F1	John Rushforth Place	D2
Avenue	D8	Douglas Street	J12	Friars Street	F6	Johnston Avenue	F2
ron Gardens	J10	(Bannockburn)		Galloway Road	F2	Johnston Street	G12
llers Court	F5	Douglas Terrace	C7	Gambeson Crescent	H10	Keir Avenue	E3
lcroft	B8	Dowan Place	C7	Gartclush Gardens	J13	Keith Avenue	G9
s Street	E8	Drip Road	C3	Gateside Road	C11, E10	Kelly Court	E5
er Street	E11	Drummond House	F7	Gillespie Place	F12	Kenningknowes Road	C8
rshall Road	E12	Drummond Place	E7	Gillies Drive	G9	Kent Road	F8
n Avenue	F1	Drummond Place	E7	Gillies Hill	B8	Kerse Road	G7, J8
olm Avenue	F2	Lane		Gladstone Place	E7	Kersebonny Road	A6
don Place	E6	Drumpark Street	F10	Glaive Avenue	H10	Kersemill Cottages	J7
don Road	E6	Duff Crescent	D4	Glasgow Road	F10	King Robert Court	C4
Street	F11	Duke Street	G12	Glebe Avenue	E6	King Street	F6
ofts Place	F7	Dumbarton Road	B5, E6	Glebe Crescent	E6	Kings Park House	D7
lls Drive	B8	Dumyat Road	F2	Glebe, The	E9	King's Park Road	E7
ore Drive	H10	Duncan Court	E3	Glen Tye Road	H8	Kings Stables Lane	E5
Road	G2	Dundas Road	F1	Glencairn Street	F10	Kirk Wynd	F9
d Road	F8	Dunster Road	G2	Glencoe Road	E4	Kirklands, The	D10
Wynd	H12	Dunvegan Drive	F2	Glendevon Drive	D3	Kirkside Crescent	F9
s Way	G13	Earlsburn Avenue	E10	Glendevon House	C3	Laburnum Grove	D8
houn Street	G7	Earlshill Drive	K12	Gogar Place	G11	Lade Mill	G12
houn Terrace	G7	East Murrayfield	J12	Goosecroft Road	F5	Ladysneuk Road	H2, H4
Park	C7	Easter Cornton Road	F1	Gordon Square	D3	Lamberton Avenue	G10
able Road	F7	Easter Livilands	G9	Gowanhill Gardens	D4	Laurel House	D7
rage Quay	G5	Easton Court	F3	Graham Avenue	G1	Laurelhill Gardens	D8
wood Drive	J13	Eccles Court	E9	Grampian Road	C7	Laurelhill Place	E7
er Close	D3	Edward Avenue	G4	Grant Place	F1	Laurencecroft Road	F3
Exchange	E6	Edward Road	F4	Graystale Road	D10	Ledi View	F2
d		Edzell Drive	F2	Greenacre Court	J12	Lennox Avenue	E9
ill Crescent	F10	Elgin Drive	G10	Greenacre Place	J13	Linden Avenue	F7
n Road	E2	Elizabeth Street	E8	Greenwood Avenue	E5	Lindsay Drive	F1
n Vale	E1	Elm Street	C4	Grendon Court	E7	Livilands Court	F8
ges		Elmbank Road	E10	Grendon Gardens	E7	Livilands Gate	F8
ne Street	E4	Endrick Place	E9	Grierson Crescent	B7	Livilands Lane	F7
Road	J12, K12	Enterprise House	J6	Haig Avenue	E3	Logie Lane	H1
ill Road	E9	Erskine Court	C3	Halberts Crescent	F11	Logie Road	H1
Crescent	H2	Esplanade	E5	Hamilton Drive	G1	Lomond Court	C3
Leith Road	H8	Etive Place	F2	Hanover Court	H1	Lomond Crescent	E1
nd Road	E10	Ewing Court	G10	Hardie Court	G10	Lomond Drive	J12
ord Drive	H13	Fairgreen Place	J13	Hart Wynd	K12	Lothian Crescent	F1
orth Crescent	D4	Fairhill Road	F12	Harvest Street	E1	Lovers Walk	F4
all Street	C4	Falconer Court	G10	Harvey Wynd	E4	Lower Bridge Street	E4

Lower Castlehill	E4	Muirhouse Road	H13	Queen Street	G11
McAllister Court	H12	Muirton Road	J7	(Bannockburn)	
MacDonald Drive	E9	Munro Avenue	F1	Queens Road	D6
McGrigor Road	E10	Munro Road	J7	Queenshaugh Drive	G4
McLaren Terrace	F10	Murnin Court	F10	Ramsay Place	E3
McLaughlan Avenue	F11	Murray Place	B8	Randolph Court	E8
MacLean Court	G10	(Cambusbarron)		Randolph Crescent	G12
MacPherson Drive	E3	Murray Place	F6	Randolph Place	G12
Mace Court	H10	(Stirling)		Randolph Road	F8
Main Street	B8	Murrayfield Place	H12	Randolph Terrace	E9
(Cambusbarron)		Murrayfield Terrace	H12	Raploch Road	D3
Main Street	E9	Murrayshall Road	F10	Renfrew Court	F2
(St Ninians)		Myreton Drive	J13	Ringans Lane	D10
Main Street	H12	Nailer Road	E11	River Wynd	D1
(Bannockburn)		Nelson Place	F7	Riverbank View	G5
Maitland Avenue	H12	New Line Road	F13	Riverside Drive	G4
Maitland Crescent	F10	New Road	H11	Robertson House	C3
Manse Crescent	E9	Newhouse	E8	Robertson Place	F10
Manse Place	J12	Newlands Road	H13	Ronald Terrace	F4
Mar Place (1)	E5	Newmarket	J12	Roseberry Place	F4
Marches, The	F6	Newpark Crescent	E11	Roseberry Terrace	F5
Margaret Road	G12	Newpark Road	E10	Ross Court	F10
Marlborough Drive	G2	North End	B7	Rowallan Drive	K13
Marschal Court	H10	North Street	H4	Rowan Court	J12
Marsden Court	H1	Oak Street	D4	Royal Gardens	E5
Maurice Avenue	H9	Ochil Crescent	E3	Royal Stuart Way	J6
Maxwell Place	F5	Ochil House	J6	Ruskie Road	F2
Maxxium House	C3	Ochil Road	G1	St Anne's Crescent	J12
Mayfield Court	F10	Ochilmount	K12	St James Orchard	H4
Mayfield Street	F9	Ochilview Mall	F6	St John Street	E5
Meadow Place	G4	Ogilvie Road	E8	St Mary's Wynd	E5
Meadows, The	F2	O'Hanlon Way	D3	St Ninians Road	C8
Meadowforth Road	G7	Old Bridge Wynd	E1	(Cambusbarron)	
Meiklejohn Street	F2	Old Drove Road	A8	St Ninians Road	E8
Melfort Drive	F9	Old Town	H12	(Laurel Hill)	
Melville Terrace	F7	Oliphant Court	F4	St Thomas's Place	C7
Mentieth Road	F2	Orchardcroft	F6	St Thomas's Well	B7
Menzies Drive	E3	Park Avenue	D7, E7	St Valery Court	D9
Middlemuir Road	G7	Park Crescent	H11	St Valery Drive	E9
Mill Hill	B8	Park Drive	H11	Sauchie Court	K12
Mill Road	B7	Park Gardens	H11	Sauchie Street	E11
Millar Place	G4	Park Lane	F5	Schiltron Way	H10
Millennium Way	C4	Park Place	D7	Scotia House	C3
Millhall Road	H9	Park Terrace	D7	Scott Street	E3
Milne Park Road	J13	Parkdyke	C7	Seaforth Place	F5
Milton Brae	F11	Parkvale Mills	B7	Seaton Drive	G9
Milton Crescent	G12	Path, The	H12	Sheriffmuirlands	G2
Milton Gardens	F12	Pelstream Avenue	F9	Shiphaugh Place	G4
Milton Grove	G13	Pelstream Court	F10	Shirra's Brae Road	F9
Milton Road	F12	Peterswell Brae	K12	Shore Road	F5
Milton Terrace	F12	Pike Road	H9	Sinclair Court	J12
Modan Road	E10	Pirnhall Road	J13	Smiddy View	B7
Montgomery Way	F2	Pitt Terrace	F6	Smillie Terrace	F2
Montrose Road	F1	Players Road	G6	Snowdon Place	D7
Monument Court	H1	Polmaise Avenue	F10	Lane	
Monument View	F3	Polmaise Court	F10	Snowdon Place	E7
Moreland Place	F2	Polmaise Road	C9, D8	South Street	H4
Morgan Court	G10	Port Street	F6	Southfield Crescent	E7
Morley Crescent	E10	Porter Avenue	F2	Spey Court	G8
Morris Terrace	E5	Pottis Road	H10	Spittal Hill	G1
Morrison Drive	G12	Princes Street	E5	Spittal Street	E6
Mossgiel Avenue	E3	Quakerfield	J12	Springbank Road	G7
Mosshouse	D9	Quarry Knowe	H13	Springfield Road	G8
Mowbrey Court	H9	Quarry Road	A8	Springkerse Road	G7
Muirend Road	F8	Queen Street	E5	Springwood	D8
Muirhead Terrace	J13	(Stirling)		Springwood Avenue	D8

Station Road		
(Stirling)		
Station Road		
(Bannockburn)		
Stein Square		
Stewart Square		
Stewart Street		
Strathallan House		
Strathmore Crescent		
Strathmore Drive		
Sunnybank Road		
Sunnyside		
Sunnyside Place		
Surcoat Loan		
Sutherland Avenue		
Sycamore Place		
Tannery Lane		
Targe Wynd		
Telford Court		
Thistle Chambers		
Thistle Place		
Thomson Place		
Torbrex Farm		
Road		
Torbrex Lane	E8
Torbrex Road		
Touch Road		
Towers Place		
Town Burn		
Underwood Cottages		
Union Street		
Upper Bridge Street		
Upper Castlehill		
Upper Craigs		
Urquhart Way		
Valley Field Place		
Victoria Place		
Victoria Road		
Victoria Square		
Viewfield Place		
Viewfield Street		
Voil Road		
Vorlich Place		
Wallace Court		
Wallace Gardens		
Wallace Gate		
Wallace Place		
Wallace Street		
(Stirling)		
Wallace Street		
(Bannockburn)		
Wallstale Road		
Waterfront Way		
Waulker Avenue		
Waverley Crescent		
Weaver Row		
Weir Street		
Wellgreen House		
Wellgreen Lane		
Wellgreen Place	F6
Wellgreen Road		
Wellgreen		
Wellpark Crescent		
West End		
West Murrayfield		
Westerlands Drive		

Index to Strathblane

thaugh Road	D1		Dunglass View	D1	
twood Crescent	F2		Edenkill Place	C2	
ns Road	F11	Ballewan Crescent	A1	Glasgow Road	A1
well Road	E4	Blairmore Cottages	D4	Kirkburn Drive	C2
ehill Place	E7	Blane Avenue	A1	Kirkburn Road	C2
ehouse Road	H7	Blane Crescent	A1	Kirkhouse Avenue	C1
am Booth Place	E10	Blane Place	A1	Kirkhouse Crescent	C1
amfield Avenue	E9	Blanefield Terrace	B1	Kirkhouse Road	C1
on Drive	G11	Campsie Dene Road	A1	Kirkland Avenue	C1
chel Place	D3	Campsie View Drive	B2	Milndavie Crescent	C2
dsor Place	E6	Cockalane View	C2	Milndavie Road	C3
nart Drive	G10	Craigenlay Avenue	C1	Milngavie Road	C2
dlands, The	F7	Craigfern Drive	C1	Moor Road	B4
dside Court	B8	Craigmarloch View	B1	Netherblane	A1
dside Road	D3	Cuilt Place	A1	New City Row	B1
lcarders Court	B7	Dumbrock Crescent	C2	Old Mugdock Road	C2
die Road	D9	Dumbrock Drive	B2	Park Place	B2
s, The	A8	Dumbrock Road	C2	Southburn Road	C2

Southview Drive	B2
Southview Road	C2
Station Lofts	C2
Station Road	A1
Strathblane Road	C2
West Row	A1
Wester Leddriegreen	B1
Road	
Wood Place	B1

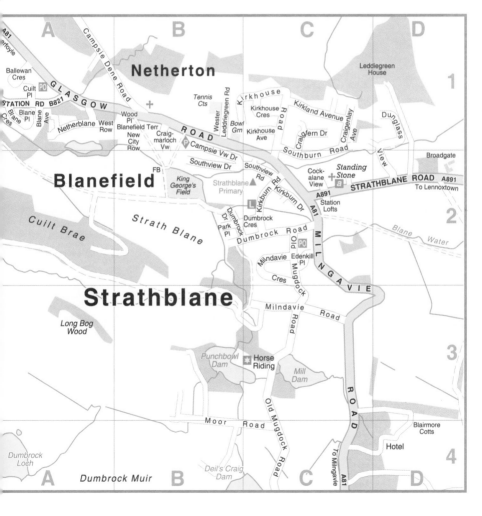

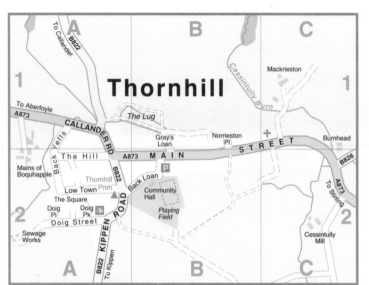

Index to Thornhill

Back Loan
Back Yetts
Callander Road
Doig Park
Doig Place
Doig Street
Grays Loan
Hill, The
Kippen Road
Low Town
Main Street
Norrieston Place
Square, The

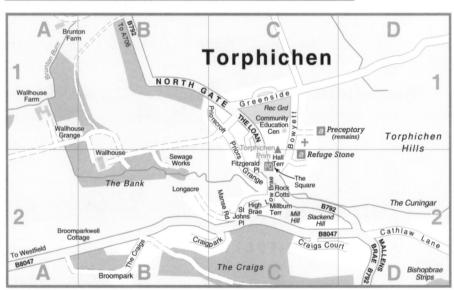

Index to Torphichen

Bowyett	C1	Greenside	C1	Millburn Terrace	C2
Broompark	B2	Hall Terrace	C2	North Gate	B1
Cathlaw Lane	D2	High Brae	C2	Priorscroft	C1
Craigpark	B2	Loan, The	C1	Priors Grange	C2
Craigs, The	B2	Low Brae	C2	Rock Cottages	C2
Craigs Court	C2	Mallens Brae	D2	St Johns Place	C2
Fitzgerald Place	C2	Manse Road	C2	Square, The	C2

Index to Westfield

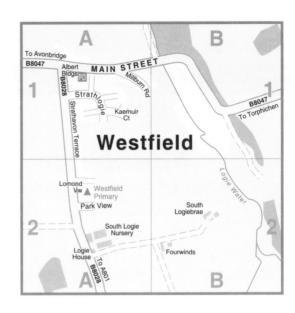

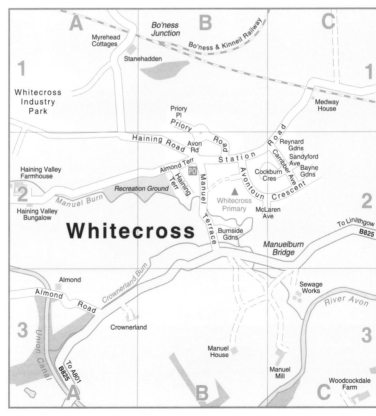

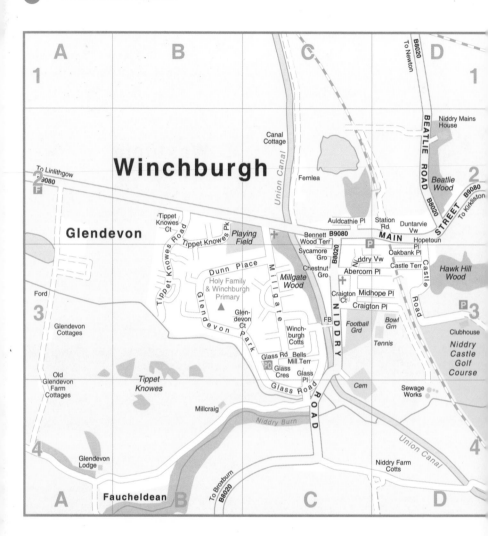

Index to Winchburgh

Abercorn Place	C3	Duntarvie View	D2	Niddry Farm Cottages	D4
Auldcathie Place	C2	Glass Crescent	C3	Niddry Road	C3
Beatlie Road	D2	Glass Place	C3	Niddry View	C3
Bells Mill Terrace	C3	Glass Road	C3, C4	Oakbank Place	D3
Bennet Wood Terrace	C2	Glendevon Cottages	A3	Old Glendevon Farm Cottages	A4
Castle Road	D3	Glendevon Court	B3	Station Road	D2
Castle Terrace	D3	Glendevon Park	B3	Sycamore Grove	C3
Chestnut Grove	C3	Hopetoun Place	D3	Tippet Knowes Court	B2
Craigton Court	C3	Main Street	D2	Tippet Knowes Park	B2
Craigton Place	C3	Midhope Place	C3	Tippet Knowes Road	B3
Dunn Place	B3	Millgate	C3	Winchburgh Cottages	C3